CREEPING CONFORMITY:
HOW CANADA BECAME SUBURBAN,
1900–1960

Creeping Conformity, the first history of suburbanization in Canada, provides a geographical perspective – both physical and social – on Canada's suburban past. Shaped by internal and external migration, decentralization of employment, and increased use of the streetcar and then the automobile, the rise of the suburb held great social promise, reflecting the aspirations of Canadian families for more domestic space and home ownership.

After 1945, however, the suburbs became stereotyped as generic, physically standardized, and socially conformist places. By 1960 they had grown further away – physically and culturally – from their respective parent cities, and brought unanticipated social and environmental consequences. Government intervention also played a key role, encouraging mortgage indebtedness, amortization, and building and subdivision regulations to become the suburban norm. Suburban homes became less affordable and more standardized, and for the first time, Canadian commentators began to speak disdainfully of 'the suburbs,' or simply 'suburbia.' *Creeping Conformity* traces how these perceptions emerged to reflect a new suburban reality.

(Themes in Canadian History)

RICHARD HARRIS is a professor in the School of Geography and Geology at McMaster University.

THEMES IN CANADIAN HISTORY

Editor: Craig Heron

RICHARD HARRIS

Creeping Conformity: How Canada Became Suburban, 1900–1960

UNIVERSITY OF TORONTO PRESS
Toronto Buffalo London

© University of Toronto Press Incorporated 2004
Toronto Buffalo London
Printed in Canada

ISBN 0-8020-3556-6 (cloth)
ISBN 0-8020-8428-1 (paper)

Printed on acid-free paper

National Library of Canada Cataloguing in Publication

Harris, Richard, 1952–
   Creeping conformity : how Canada became suburban,
   1900–1960 / Richard Harris.

   (Themes in Canadian history)
   Includes bibliographical references and index.
   ISBN 0-8020-3556-6 (bound)   ISBN 0-8020-8428-1 (pbk.)

   1. Suburbs – Canada – History.   2. Suburban life – Canada –
   History.   3. Housing policy – Canada – History.   I. Title.
   II. Series.

   HT352.C3H37 2004   307.74'0971   C2004-900166-3

University of Toronto Press acknowledges the financial
assistance to its publishing program of the Canada Council
for the Arts and the Ontario Arts Council.

University of Toronto Press acknowledges the financial
support for its publishing activities of the Government of
Canada through the Book Publishing Industry Development
Program (BPIDP).

Contents

FIGURES   vii

ACKNOWLEDGMENTS   ix

1 Introduction   3

2 A Place and a People   18

3 Cities and Suburbs   46

4 The Making of Suburban Diversity, 1900–1929   74

5 The Growing Influence of the State   106

6 The Rise of the Corporate Suburb, 1945–1960   129

7 Creeping Conformity?   155

BIBLIOGRAPHY   175

INDEX   193

Figures

1 Vancouver in 1930   4
2 Shaughnessy Heights, Vancouver, in 1926   21
3 The home of Pierre Vallières, Longeuil, Quebec   44
4 The plan for Coldbrook Garden City, Saint John, New Brunswick, 1913   47
5 Manufacturing districts in Montreal, 1935   59
6 Toronto in the 1920s   61
7 Aerial view of west Edmonton, 1924   65
8 Subdivision advertisement for The Uplands, Victoria, 1912   86
9 Speculatively built interwar housing in Westdale, Hamilton   95
10 Different builders produced varied streetscapes, east Toronto, 1920s   97
11 House building in suburban Windsor, Ontario   118
12 Model home display, Eaton's, Calgary, 1948   122
13 Park Royal, West Vancouver, 1962   131
14 Institutional mortgage finance in Hamilton, 1951   135
15 The post-war suburb, Lethbridge, Alberta, 1951   139

Acknowledgments

The argument in this book has evolved over a number of years. It rests upon research that has been supported on several occasions by the Social Sciences and Humanities Research Council, and my first thanks must be to successive council committees and through them to the Canadian taxpayer for their assistance. Authors have a responsibility to their audience – to be clear, concise, and reliable – but this is especially true when that audience has unwittingly paid in advance.

Over the years a number of colleagues and students have contributed ideas, information, and understanding. I would especially like to thank A. Victoria Bloomfield (may she rest in peace), Doris Forrester (née Ragonetti), Ken Jackson, Robert Lewis, Larry McCann, Ted Relph, Matt Sendbuehler, Tricia Shulist, Mary Sies, and John Weaver, as well as two anonymous readers. Michael Buzzelli, John Hagopian, Michael Mercier, and Carolyn Whitzman offered valuable suggestions on an earlier draft. Robert Lewis, Larry McCann, and Graeme Wynn helped to make and/or locate illustrations.

Like everyone, my view of suburbs has been shaped by my own experience. For fifteen years I have lived in a Hamilton neighbourhood that was once a suburb and is still suburban in terms of density, dwelling type, and tenure. The members of my own family, Carol, Alex, and

Peter, have in their different ways encouraged me to reflect on what this partly suburban experience means. To them I owe my deepest thanks and love, and so to them I dedicate this book.

CREEPING CONFORMITY:
HOW CANADA BECAME SUBURBAN,
1900–1960

1

Introduction

... there's no there, there.
Gertrude Stein, speaking of Oakland, a suburb

In the late 1920s the carpenter Arthur Evans built a house for himself, his wife, and their infant daughter Jean at 27 East 42nd Avenue in South Vancouver. This was suburban territory, although soon to be annexed by the City of Vancouver. The location was good, only a few steps from the stop on Main Street from which they could take a streetcar downtown. They would have heard the rumble on the rails as they had breakfast. Within a few years, however, disaster struck. The onset of the Great Depression in the fall of 1929 was devastating enough. Then, in September 1933, Evans was imprisoned for his vocal opposition to the 'do-nothing' provincial government. Without Arthur's wages, the family could not maintain payments on their $1,800 mortgage, which was owed to Alderman Twiss. Twiss foreclosed and the sheriff served an eviction order on 19 March 1934. There was a protracted battle, during which organizations of workers and the unemployed manned pickets at the Evans's home. Offering twenty-four-hour support, many slept in the front room and the basement. Eventually, on 24 April twenty carloads of police, backed by eight men on horseback and six on motorcycles, evicted Mrs Evans and her daughter. Jean was in Grade 1.

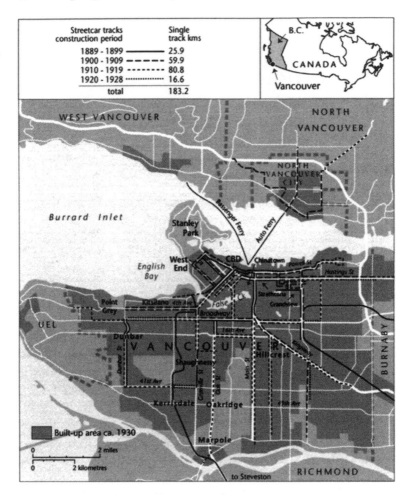

Streetcar tracks construction period		Single track kms
1889 - 1899	——————	25.9
1900 - 1909	— — — — —	59.9
1910 - 1919	··········	80.8
1920 - 1928	················	16.6
total		183.2

1   Vancouver in 1930 at the end of three decades of rapid suburban growth. In 1929 the city had annexed extensive suburbs, including Point Grey and South Vancouver, where Arthur Evans lived on 42nd Avenue near Main Street. Urban development still reflected the influence of streetcars, although automobiles were beginning to have an impact. (Courtesy of Graeme Wynn and Eric Leinberger)

None of the elements of this story seems typical. Canadians, including many scholars, suppose that suburban
houses have always been constructed by professional builders and developers, not by people for their own use, and
that suburbs were occupied by the families of the middle
and upper classes, not by the likes of Arthur Evans. They
have also assumed that, burdened by mortgages and preoc-
cupied with family matters, suburban house owners have
been a conservative lot. In the mid-1990s a Conservative
government came to power in Ontario by sweeping the
so-called 905 region – a reference to the common tele-
phone code shared by the belt of affluent outer suburbs
that ring Toronto. So close was the association between
politics and place that, in order to understand Ontario pre-
mier Mike Harris's 'common sense revolution,' the
reporter Stephen Dale ventured into the cappuccino bars
and muffler shops of darkest Aurora, a prosperous town
now joined to Toronto by urban sprawl. His report, *Lost in
the Suburbs*, uses sprawl as a metaphor for modern life.

If a conservative lifestyle of domestic consumerism has
been one type of suburban experience, there have also
been others. For example, in the early decades of the century, and again after the Second World War, hundreds of
thousands of Canadians built their own houses. Many suburbs, including parts of the urban fringe around every
Canadian city, were settled by immigrants and blue-collar
workers. Especially during the 1930s and 1940s, a large
number of these suburbs fostered or supported left-wing
politics. Several examples make the point. In 1935 Arthur
Evans led the On-to-Ottawa-Trek, one of the most significant events in the history of Canadian labour. In February
1942 the residents of Toronto's northwestern suburbs
elected Joseph Noseworthy as the first member of Parlia-
ment in Ontario for the Cooperative Commonwealth
Federation (CCF), the socialist precursor to the New Democratic Party (NDP). In Quebec, similar districts nurtured
radical separatists. The autobiographical sections of *White*

Niggers of America show that the post-war shacktowns of
Montreal's suburban south shore shaped the thinking of
Pierre Vallières, a leading Quebec separatist in the 1970s.
Just as much as the gracious, comfortable avenues of suburban mythology, such places and experiences have been
part of the story of Canadian suburbs. In contrast to their
supposed singularity, the initial diversity of the suburbs is a
point of departure of this book, its first and major theme.

It is important to understand both the myth and the reality of the suburbs because Canada has became a suburban
nation. Statistics reveal the bare bones of the story. In 1900
very few Canadians lived in what contemporaries would
have regarded as suburbs. Slightly more than one-third of
the nation lived in urban areas, the great majority city-
dwellers. By 1960 suburbanites, as they had come to be
known, were widespread: three-fifths of the nation lived
in urban areas, the majority of whom lived in suburbs,
broadly defined, while many more aspired to live there. In
the first three decades of this century, suburban living had
ceased to be unusual; by the end of another three decades
it had become the social norm. In this book I tell the story
of how that transformation was accomplished and of how it
affected the lives of many Canadians.

The transformation of Canada into a suburban nation
eventually led to a suppression of diversity. In the early
decades of the century suburbs were built by a variety of
means and were settled by all kinds of people. No one
thought to lump them together under a single label. By
1960 people spoke freely of 'the Canadian suburb.' Suburbs were being created in standard ways, and those who
bought into them lived a fundamentally similar way of life.
In part, this change simply reflected the fact that, having
become unaffordable to those on low incomes, the post-
war suburbs contained a narrower range of classes. More
important, there had been a convergence in the living standards and priorities of a broad mass of working-class and
middle-class families. This merge entailed both a gain and

a loss. Crucial changes were provoked by government initiatives in the field of housing finance from the mid-1930s onward. Within a broadly chronological framework, then, in this book I tell a story of creeping conformity, not only of the suburbs but also of certain aspects of Canadian society. I sketch the methods of suburb-making that prevailed up to 1929 (chapter 4), the evolution of state intervention after the mid-1930s (chapter 5), and the emergence of new corporate suburbs after 1945 (chapter 6).

The rise of the suburbs is more than the story of how they were developed. Suburbs are usually defined in physical terms, commonly as residential districts with low densities that are located at, or near, the urban fringe. Many observers, however, have been equally interested in their social characteristics. *Suburbanites* is the sometimes disdainful term that became popular in the middle decades of the twentieth century to describe the kind of people who live in suburbs. The term has become unfashionable, but the concept lives on. Suburbanites are thought to value privacy and domesticity, to have turned their backs on the city and, by implication, those who are less fortunate than themselves. In *The Suburban Society*, the sociologist S.D. Clark describes the social life of the 1950s suburbs, where 'families turned in towards themselves ... not a society in which people were alert to the important issues of the world.' Increasingly, over the course of the twentieth century, the residents of suburbs have also come to be seen as addicted consumers, buying houses, furnishings, cars, appliances, clothing, fast food, and much else besides, leading a lifestyle of private consumerism. If this perception is true, then the rise of the suburbs must have entailed a steady change in the way that Canadians live and think. Interwoven with the story of how suburbs were created are arguments about what the rise of the suburbs has meant. In chapter 2 the two-way relationship that has always existed between the physical character of the suburban place and way of life of its residents is disentangled. In chapter 4 I show how

diverse suburbs once were, especially before the Second
World War, while in chapter 7 I explore the ways that suburban families have lived, tracing continuities, as well as the
rise of a new conformity, over the first sixty years of the century.

The dates that I have used to frame this story are mean-
ingful, although to some degree arbitrary. Suburbanization
began before 1900. In the larger cities, quite extensive suburbs had grown up during prosperous decades from the
1840s onward. In Montreal in the 1850s, for example,
impressive terraces were built on newly subdivided lots
north of Dorchester Street, between Mountain and University streets, while above Sherbrooke Street estates were laid
out on the lower slopes of Mount Royal. Similarly, during
the economic boom of the 1880s another fine suburb
began to grow up in Toronto north of Bloor Street and
west of Avenue Road, an area that became known as the
Annex after it was brought into the city in 1884. But the
wave of suburban growth that gathered momentum after
1900 was different, above all in scale. The depression of
the 1890s was the deepest of the nineteenth century, in
some respects equalling that of the Great Depression of the
1930s. Some cities lost population for a short time in the
1890s, and few new houses were built. In areas like the
Annex, which had been subdivided but incompletely developed during the 1880s, the discontinuity was blurred:
piecemeal development in the 1900s filled in the gaps.
Much more striking was the creation of extensive new districts during the speculative boom in suburban subdivision
that reached a fever between 1909 and 1912.

Subdivisions that were laid out between 1900 and 1914
produced suburbs on a wholly new scale around almost
every Canadian city. Two developments combined to create
this new phenomenon: the electric streetcar and unprecedented population growth. Except in suburbs that provide
a significant number of jobs, the nature and extent of suburban development is constrained by how far people are

able to commute. In the nineteenth century, the great majority of people walked to work. Only a small minority of professionals and businessmen could afford to travel by horse cars, which had become established by the 1870s. As long as most jobs were located in or near the downtown, there were tight limits as to how far from them most people could live. The electric streetcar did not abolish these limits, but it did greatly extend them. It was much cheaper for passengers than the horse car and, except in the congested central districts, it was also much faster. Perhaps by 1910, and certainly by the 1920s, it had become affordable to the majority of workers. The impact of the streetcar was highlighted by the fact that it was adopted in every major Canadian city at almost exactly the same time: in the first half of the 1890s. The effects became apparent when prosperity, and with it immigration rates, picked up after the turn of the century. During the boom that preceded the First World War immigration rates soared to levels that have never again been equalled, either in relative or even in absolute terms. Some immigrants settled in rural areas, but most found work in cities. The population of Canada increased by 34 per cent between 1901 and 1911, but the majority of the increase occurred in urban areas, which grew by more than 60 per cent. The greatest rates of growth occurred in the largest centres, Toronto and Montreal, which more than doubled in size in that decade. These cities, rather than the smaller centres where people could continue to walk to work, were exactly where the streetcar could have its greatest effect.

In western cities, notably Calgary and Edmonton and to a lesser extent Winnipeg and Vancouver, streetcar lines were extended outwards into undeveloped territory. They were viewed as a promotional instrument, boosting not only the value of particular parcels and strips of land but also the population potential of the city as a whole. In eastern cities, including Montreal and especially Toronto, the private companies that at first ran the streetcar lines tended to be more cautious about building tracks into areas that had few paying customers. Indeed, the Toronto Railway Company was quite obdurate on this point, forcing the city to build lines to service some of the newer areas. Even in Toronto, however, the availability of a new means of transportation within the built-up area encouraged speculators to buy and subdivide land beyond the city limits. The result was an unprecedented orgy of speculation and development that scattered hundreds of subdivisions and tens of thousands of building lots across the suburban bush. Suburban development on a new scale was born. Moreover, since the western cities were so young, it was the first wave of suburban development of truly national scope. In many ways, then, 1900 marked the beginning of a new suburban era.

It is less easy to know when to end the story. Suburban development continues, and the proportion of people living in suburbs grows daily. But for several decades now growth has not been accompanied by significant change. Arguably, by the late 1950s the peculiar character of modern-day suburbs had been established. Produced by large land developers, they are affordable only through highly leveraged debt. How they look is determined by the general requirements of the automobile and has come to be specified by national building codes, zoning, and subdivision requirements. Since all these elements were firmly in place by 1960, that is when I have chosen to end my account.

A key development was a new system of home financing. Until the Great Depression, most Canadians had not relied to any great extent upon mortgages. Many saved up until they could afford to build or buy. The Evans family had taken out a mortgage after their house was finished, and only because Arthur wanted to make some money by building and selling another house. Like Evans, most borrowers obtained money from another individual, not a lending institution. Typically, they had to find a down payment of

50 per cent or more and were able to borrow for no more than five years, and even then only in the form of so-called balloon mortgages, loans on which the borrower paid only interest. At the end of the term of the loan the borrower had to repay the original principal as a lump sum or else refinance, which could be difficult during an economic downturn. In 1935 the federal government passed the Dominion Housing Act (DHA) under which, in conjunction with 'approved' lenders, it offered a new type of mortgage. It provided for more extensive borrowing (at least 60 per cent of value, a much longer-term (twenty and soon twenty-five years), and a system of amortization by which borrowers repaid both interest and principal under a system of blended payments. Through DHA mortgages, which became NHA mortgages under a new National Housing Act in 1938, mortgage insurance also was offered. This type of mortgage has become standard, but it was slow to catch on. In the late 1930s fewer than 10 per cent of new houses were built under the auspices of the DHA/NHA. In the late 1940s this proportion rose to about a third and by the mid-1950s to about two-fifths. It was not until 1958, however, that more than half of all new homes in urban areas were built under the auspices of the NHA. From about this date, then, we can say that a new method of building and financing the suburbs, and hence a new way of living, was put in place.

Less tangible but perhaps more important, it was during the 1950s that Canadians – along with Americans and Australians – came to think of the suburbs as a fundamental part of their national experience. In earlier decades journalists and social observers had written about suburbs. It was only in the 1950s, however, that they began to view the suburbs generically, as a national phenomenon and as a mirror of the nation. The new way of thinking was most clearly expressed in the United States. Builders were represented as national heroes, and the families that settled there were defined as the social norm. In July 1950, for example, *Time* magazine chose William Levitt, builder of three huge suburban communities, as Man of the Year. Soon, the best-known couple in North America, Lucy and Ricky Ricardo, moved out of their downtown New York apartment and into the Los Angeles suburbs. The symbolism was obvious and immediately established a sitcom norm. American academics such as David Reissman and William Whyte dissected the suburbs, convinced that it was there that they would find clues to what was happening in the larger national culture. The suburbs had become the site and symbol of the American future.

Canadians were also coming to think of suburban families as both the norm and the ideal. In 1954 *Maclean's* magazine ran a story by John Gray that claimed to offer 'the facts on the great migration that has changed the face of Canada from coast to coast.' Sitcoms such as *I Love Lucy* and *Leave It to Beaver* had as much resonance for Canadians as for Americans. Canadian scholars such as John Seeley wrote about suburbs in the same way as Americans did, assuming that they were the laboratories in which social observers might discover the mores that were shaping the nation. Americans accepted this assessment at face value. Published in 1956, Seeley, Sim, and Loosley's study of Forest Hill, Toronto (thinly disguised as 'Crestwood Heights'), was introduced by David Reissman as another study to be added to the rapidly growing bookshelf on North American suburbs. The latter half of the 1950s was not the end of the suburban story, but it was the end of a chapter, a period when the suburbs as we know them first rose to national prominence. It marked the end of the rise of the suburbs.

Although the rise of the suburbs has had important social consequences, its study has not been the exclusive concern of social historians. Indeed, most of those who have written about this history have been urbanists, primarily historians such as John Weaver and Donald Davis or historical geographers such as Larry McCann and Robert Lewis. This point has mattered because urban scholars and social historians tend to have different interests. One group has been interested in showing how suburbs have developed and with what consequences for the landscape, while the other has depicted features of the lives of suburban families, especially women. Because only a few Canadian social historians have shown a specific interest in the suburbs, we know more about how suburbs developed than about the lives of their residents. More important, neither urban scholars nor social historians have consistently tried to understand the relationship between social life and physical space. One group typically follows the story to the point where houses have been built; the other takes the dwelling for granted. In order to understand the full meaning of the rise of the suburbs, their two aspects – house and home, place and people – must be viewed as an interrelated whole. This relationship, often complex and still in many respects obscure, constitutes the second major theme of this book.

One of the reasons why social historians have paid little attention to suburbs is that they usually define their interests in terms of specific issues, such as feminism, or of social groups, whether workers, women, children, immigrants, or racialized minorities. From this point of view, suburbs may seem to be just one of the places in which any of these issues or groups may be found, so that the suburban setting becomes incidental. This is true, for example, of Franca Iacovetta's study of delinquent 'bad girls' in suburban Toronto in the 1950s. She does not suggest that there was anything uniquely suburban about the experience of this group: social variables frame her analysis. At most, she probes the social stereotype of the 1950s suburb as uniformly conformist and acquiescent. Indeed, the suburban label is sometimes used in a mainly metaphorical way to invoke a social stereotype. In *Roughing It in the Suburbs*, an analysis of the politics of *Chatelaine* magazine in the 1950s and 1960s, Valerie Korinek alludes briefly to the diversity of early post-war suburbs but never connects this

diversity with her theme. Even when a particular suburb is
the site of a case study, its peculiar character as a suburb
may be forgotten unless the researcher makes a deliberate
effort to address the issue. Thus, for example, Suzanne
Morton's account of family life in a working-class suburb of
Halifax in the 1920s speaks eloquently of class, gender, and
age, but not so much of place. All are valuable studies in
their own way, but they do not illuminate how, or require
us to believe that, suburban residence has entailed a distinctive way of life. Although the early diversity and changing character of the suburbs has sometimes made the task
difficult, in this book I try to clarify the exact nature of this
distinctiveness.

   The story of the suburbs can throw light on the history of
domesticity and the nuclear family, since suburbs are their
clearest embodiment. It is equally essential to the history of
women and childhood. Suburbs have always been seen as
places for women and children even when, as in some fem-
inist writing, this allocation has not necessarily been viewed
as a good thing. Arguably, the rise of suburbs has had an
equally significant impact upon men, upon the nature of
their engagement with family life and with the competing
demands of work and workplace politics. Those who have
considered this issue have generally supposed that suburban living has tempered labour militancy, but, as I have
already suggested, this has not always been true. The linkages are contingent. Suburbs should also figure in the history of immigrants, although in different ways depending
upon the period, place, and group in question. The stereotype is that immigrants settled first in central ghettoes. In
later moving to the suburbs they are supposed to have signalled their social mobility as well as their integration into
Canadian life. This is the way that things worked for some
groups, but not for all, and such differences in residential
experience surely mattered. Paying attention to the way in
which the rise of the suburbs has intersected the lives of
various social groups, in this book I suggest how the history

of the suburbs can illuminate a number of other themes in Canadian social history.

If the history of the suburbs cuts across many other themes in Canadian history, it is also distinctive in the gap that exists between scholarly writing and popular experience. Historians of the family, labour, women, and immigrants usually have a basic sympathy for their subject and have often spoken for as well as about it. In contrast, those who have written about suburbs, including writers and reporters as well as academics, have frequently expressed scorn for their subject. In a piece for *Maclean's* in 1954 the Canadian writer Hugh Garner relieved himself of a considerable quantity of bile on the subject under the title 'You Take the Suburbs ... I Don't Want Them.' Two decades later Humphrey Carver, a British immigrant and perhaps the most influential planner in the early post-war years, described Canadian suburbs as 'unexpectedly horrible ... impersonal, synthetic, exchangeable, temporary.' With a fastidious disdain typical of the academic writer, British historian F.M.L. Thompson has commented of the suburb that 'it is not necessary to admire it in order to wish to understand how it happened.' These prejudices have been widespread. As recently as 1999 Rosalyn Baxandall and Elizabeth Ewen, authors of *Picture Windows,* a well-reviewed book about post-war suburbs in the United States, confessed that they had begun their research with a strong predisposition against the suburbs, even though they taught there. Through this rhetorical device they were surely trying to defuse, by anticipating, the criticism of their professional colleagues. At the same time, it is clear that for many decades the suburbs are exactly where most North Americans have wished to live. As James Lorimer admitted rather ruefully in *The Developers,* his account of the post-war development industry, the only criticism offered by most Canadian families about the post-war suburbs has been the cost of entry. A historian of Canadian suburbs must recognize the strength of feeling on both sides and make an attempt to reconcile what can appear to be unrecognizably different accounts of the same thing. The continuing dialogue between critic and advocate, the chattering and the popular classes, constitutes a third theme of the book.

A particular suburb is a place, in the same sense that Quebec City, say, is a place. But 'suburbs' are a different type of place from, for example, 'provinces' or 'regions.' Regions are – in varying degrees but by their very definition – unique. Suburbs are – in varying degrees but by definition – generic. To speak of Shaughnessy Heights and South Vancouver as suburbs is to imply that they have something in common; it is to highlight that commonality. In the early decades of the twentieth century, when both of these areas were developing, suburbs were more diverse than they have become. Since the Second World War, suburbs across the country have become more similar, most obviously in the manner that they are financed and built. At the same time, they have become more like those in the United States, and indeed elsewhere. Until the Second World War, Canada was a less urban, and hence a less suburban, nation than the United States. In the first two decades after 1945 Canadians caught up. In the process we rapidly adopted methods of land subdivision and home financing that had developed earlier south of the border. By the 1960s suburbs in Canada and the United States appeared and felt more similar than ever. For that reason, it has become increasingly useful not only to compare the Canadian experience with that of the United States but, on issues where Canadian research is meagre or non-existent, to use American findings to provide insights into the Canadian experience. I have done so sparingly, chiefly in chapter 2, in which the relationship between suburbs and their inhabitants are explored in a general way.

It is impossible not to see the past through the eyes of the present. Our own social experience presses in upon us, offering assumptions and preoccupations, together with a vocabulary with which to apprehend the world as we know it. This is perhaps especially true when we look at suburbs, which are so tangible. It is not simply that 'suburb' has a particular meaning in our own time but, omnipresent, the modern suburb can seem both inevitable and immutable. A history of suburbs can so readily be framed as an account of how the modern suburb came into being. Such histories have been written. A good example is Marc Weiss's *The Rise of the Community Builders*, which is the story of how, in U.S. metropolitan areas, the ideas and practices of large land developers eventually came to dominate. Focusing on the first half of the twentieth century, Weiss does an effective job of showing how the self-styled community builders formulated their ideas and gained influence. In the process, however, he offers an incomplete picture of how most suburbs of that period were being developed. The same is true of James Lorimer, who, in tracing the operations of the Canadian development industry, paid little attention to the other forms of land development and house building that for many years remained common. Similar comments might be made about attempts to trace the rise to dominance of those social assumptions and practices that are most fully embodied in the suburbs, for example, the nuclear family and privatized forms of consumption. It is important to recover the past that gets overlooked in this sort of narrative, not only in the interests of historical completeness or accuracy. If we really want to understand why we live the way we do, we need to know the alternatives that have been supplanted, and why. By emphasizing the diversity of Canadian suburbs, it becomes easier to give due weight to the approaches to making and inhabiting suburbs that have now become quite rare.

2

A Place and a People

... we make our surroundings, and then our surroundings make us: and at the moment they are a working model of hell.
Norman Pearson, 'Hell Is a Suburb'

As a society, we have made our suburbs. They express our values, not to mention our bank accounts, and offer symbols and clues to our cultural experiences: the mall, the cul-de-sac, and the detached house, lately with a two- (or three-) car garage. Many writers argue that suburbs are not only expressive but influential, that they have shaped us, though not necessarily in the ways that we have intended, or even desired. It is, above all, because suburbs can affect the way we live that we need to take seriously their growth and ubiquity. The nature of their influence is diffuse and subtle, however, and to understand it we need to look at what, exactly, a suburb is.

The Physical Characteristics of Suburbs

Today suburbs are built around cars, but this was not always the case. What are the more enduring features of the suburb? Scholars, and Canadians in general, have usually identified six criteria, although in varying combinations:

1 low density of development, typically of detached, or semi-detached, dwellings

2 location at, or close to, the urban fringe
3 high level of owner-occupation
4 politically distinct
5 middle, or upper-middle class in character
6 exclusively residential, implying that residents must commute beyond the suburb to work.

Some of these six criteria are related, in particular through the economics of the land market. Land in fringe areas is comparatively cheap, making it possible for many families to own detached houses on large lots. Other criteria, however, are only contingently connected. In large cities, where jobs are concentrated in or near the city centre, it is likely that only people in middle-class occupations can afford the expense of long commutes from suburban homes. In smaller centres, however, or where jobs are not confined to the centre, a large majority of families may be able to afford detached houses at the urban fringe.

At some point, every urban district today has met at least one of these criteria: fringe location. Many have met several, but very few have satisfied all six. The challenge, then, is to decide whether any are of critical importance and, if not, to establish how many criteria have to be satisfied for a place to count as suburban. There is no single, correct answer to this question. Not only have nations developed different types of suburbs, but also they have conceived of suburbs in different ways. Depending upon their particular purposes, those who have written about suburbs have found it useful to define the scope of their enquiries more or less narrowly. In order to determine and rationalize a view that is useful for present purposes, it is necessary to be guided not only by the logic of what others have written, but also by the nature of the Canadian experience. If a definition will determine what we include within a history of Canadian suburbs, it is important that we allow that history – including the ways in which Canadians in general have viewed the suburbs – to guide our thinking.

Some writers have insisted that almost all criteria must be

met in order for a district to qualify as suburban. For example, in *Bourgeois Utopias*, Robert Fishman has traced the history of the middle-class suburban ideal from its British roots in the late eighteenth century to its more general North American development in the late nineteenth and early twentieth centuries. He argues that, inspired by the rural estates of the aristocracy, it was the bourgeoisie that created and occupied the first suburbs; thus, he sees the archetypal suburb as residential and middle class. Indeed, he argues that because post-war suburbs have typically been accessible to a wide spectrum of the population and have incorporated industrial and office parks as well as major shopping centres, they are no longer 'true' suburbs. For Fishman, the long rise of the suburbs was followed, in the latter half of the twentieth century, by a more rapid fall. Fishman makes no reference to Canadian examples, but it would be easy to illustrate his argument with prestigious districts such as Westmount, Outremont, and Mount Royal (Montreal); Rosedale, Lawrence Park, and Forest Hill (Toronto); Tuxedo Park (Winnipeg); Shaughnessy Heights and Point Grey (Vancouver); and the Uplands (Victoria). The influence may also be seen in more socially mixed districts, such as Hamilton's Westdale, or on a smaller scale, as in Dickson's Hill in Galt, Ontario. Laid out between the 1880s and the 1930s, all these areas express a middle-class, Anglo-American ideal of fine homes located in graciously planned areas, of green retreats from the rigours of work: a happy marriage of city and country. All are quite visible, not only locally but in some cases at the national level. They are the kind of places about which histories are written, and they figure prominently in the historiography of Canadian suburbs.

When North Americans speak about suburbs, they almost always are speaking of places that cannot meet such exclusive social standards. In *Crabgrass Frontier*, his influential history of U.S. suburbs, the historian Kenneth Jackson sets out to survey low-density, residential areas that were

2   Shaughnessy Heights, Vancouver, in 1926. Designed in 1908 by the
Olmsted company on land owned by the CPR, Shaughnessy Heights
exemplified a suburban ideal of gracious exclusivity in a semi-rural setting. It was typical of only one type of Canadian suburb. (National Air
Photo Library. B.A. 10.23)

occupied by middle- and upper-income homeowners. As is
typical among Americans, however, Jackson defines 'middle' very broadly to include the families of skilled and semi-
skilled workers. Indeed, he implies that home ownership
itself may be regarded as a sign of middle-class status. This
does not quite sit comfortably with Canadians, who, to
some extent following the British tradition, still think of
social class as being established in the workplace. But Jackson's broader definition of suburbs is closer to the normal
Canadian usage than that of Fishman. It would include, for
example, most of the residential areas in what are usually
referred to as the post-war suburbs. The pockets of high-

rise public housing, built mostly during the 1960s, are arguably an exception.

In one important respect, Americans and Canadians
have differed in the way that they think about suburbs. For
Americans, to be a suburb a place usually must have its own
political identity, its own municipal government. Canadians
recognize that political identities matter, but they have not
regarded it as a decisive issue. In this, too, they seem to have
been influenced by British precedents. As Richard Harris
and Peter Larkham have shown, national differences have
been reflected not only in the historiography of suburbs in
each country but also in the definitions offered in their dic-
tionaries. The main reason why Canadians have placed less
emphasis upon political identity is constitutional. In the
United States, the powers of local governments are set out in
the constitution; they cannot be made, or unmade, by the
states. In Canada, local governments have no powers other
than those the provinces choose to delegate. Provincial governments have the power to amalgamate local governments
without the permission of the municipalities in question, a
power that has been exercised on a number of occasions.
Despite municipal opposition, the Province of Ontario created a metropolitan level of government for Toronto in
1953 and then in 1998 amalgamated the city with the five
metropolitan suburbs. Effective 1 January 2002, the Province of Quebec forced the amalgamation of the City of
Montreal with all suburbs on the island, of Quebec City with
its suburbs, and of the municipalities on the Quebec side of
the national capital region, including Hull, Aylmer, and
Gatineau. Thus, in the United States, but not in Canada,
independent political status has been a plausible and important source of identity for suburban residents.

Setting aside political status as a requirement, it is still
clear that even a relatively broad definition of suburbs,
such as that articulated by Kenneth Jackson, excludes
much of what has happened at the urban fringe. Most obviously, it excludes all non-residential land use and fringe

residential areas that developed in close proximity to industrial or commercial workplaces. This is not a minor matter. In the late nineteenth century it was common for homes and industry to grow up cheek by jowl. This pattern was most apparent in areas located in and around the city core, but it was also common in the numerous situations where factories were established at the urban fringe. As Robert Lewis has shown, it occurred repeatedly outside Montreal, for example, in Verdun. It was also apparent around Toronto in West Toronto Junction (1880s–), New Toronto (1890s–), York Township (1900s–), and to a lesser extent Leaside (1910s–); it characterized east, and also parts of southwest Hamilton, as well as Point Douglas and nearby sections of Winnipeg's North End (1900s-). Such places did not look, sound, or smell, like Westmount or Rosedale, but they were regarded as suburban. To refer to them, contemporaries coined the term 'industrial suburb.' This implied that such places were a common feature of the suburban scene, as indeed they were.

Most industrial suburbs grew up as separate municipalities, but this was not always true, and many were soon annexed by the adjacent city. In terms of the six criteria listed above, therefore, they consistently satisfied only one requirement: location at the urban fringe. If they should be regarded as suburban, then so, too, must the owner-built residential suburbs of workers and immigrants. As I have suggested in *Unplanned Suburbs*, and as Arthur Evans's experience indicates, they were a fixture on the suburban scene around most Canadian cities from the 1900s to the early 1950s. Even using the broadest definition of middle class, they would not qualify as suburban according to the fifth criterion listed above. Indeed, they were often referred to as 'shacktowns,' which was an unfair label, since their residents usually improved them to the level of stable, self-respecting communities, even if it did sometimes take years and was accomplished in a haphazard fashion. But contemporaries had no difficulty in regarding them as suburban places.

In 1914 Alice Randle reported her visit to one of Toronto's shacktowns in a piece that she wrote for *Saturday Night* magazine. She entitled her article quite simply, 'Suburban Settlement.' In so doing she may have intended a hint of irony – she made it clear that she supposed such suburbs would be unfamiliar to her readers – but her defence of the motives and accomplishments of these strange suburbanites was wholehearted. Half a century later, when S.D. Clark surveyed the suburban scene around Toronto, he included all types of settlement, from the affluent sections of Don Mills to shack districts in Scarborough and East Gwillimbury Township. Criticizing the way in which most academics had chosen to study the expensive, 'packaged' subdivisions, he insisted that suburbs took many forms. John Gray had made the same point in *Maclean's* in 1954. In his illustrated article a series of pictures of an idyllic Don Mills was counterbalanced with another series showing tar-paper shacks in Ville Jacques Cartier on the suburban south shore of Montreal. He may have implied that one was superior to the other, but he did not question that both were suburbs.

In Canada, gracious, exclusive places such as Shaughnessy have perhaps been regarded as the height of suburbia, but not as its essence. Canadians generally have not chosen to define suburbs in terms of class, or even in terms of a purely residential character. Instead, they have spoken about density of settlement, building type, and often home ownership, while acknowledging that in some contexts political identity has also mattered. Above all, Canadians have consistently emphasized the importance of location at, or near, the developing urban fringe. I will follow their lead.

The Social Characteristics of Suburbs

Writers have often seen the physical features of the suburbs as expressions of a distinctively suburban way of life. An example is the way that the visual monotony of new subdivisions has been interpreted as a sign of social conformity. Thus, F.M.L. Thompson summarizes the way in which contemporaries viewed English suburbs in the period up to 1939: 'The suburbs appeared monotonous, featureless, without character,' he observes, 'indistinguishable from one another, infinitely boring to behold, wastelands of housing as settings for dreary, petty lives without social, cultural, or intellectual interests, settings which fostered a pretentious preoccupation with outward appearances, a fussy attention to the trifling details of genteel living, and absurd attempts to conjure rusticity out of minute garden plots.' Some elements of this harangue – 'fussy,' 'garden plots' – seem very English, and Thompson's suggestion that suburbs seemed indistinguishable does not have resonance in Canada in the early decades of this century. But its spirit certainly informed the North American discourse about suburbs after 1945. In *Maclean's* in 1954, for example, John Gray described repetitive 'strawberry boxes and ranch-style bungalows' and offered an anecdote about the neighbours who repainted a man's house while he was away on holiday, because they thought the existing colour scheme was discordant. The interrelation between social outlook and physical appearance often seemed too obvious to need underlining. In the late 1950s Malvina Reynolds's song 'Little Boxes' was a popular hit in Canada as well as the United States. Reynolds condemned the 'boxes' made of 'ticky-tacky.' Hearing that song, no one doubted that the concluding refrain – 'and they all look just the same' – referred equally to the homes and their occupants.

The most common view concerning the relationship of social process and suburban form is that suburban landscapes have directly reflected the tastes of their residents. The detached single-family home is seen to reflect a preferred, private, family-centred style of life. It allows for a public display of taste and wealth while encouraging an essential privacy. The occupants of such a house can show their wealth through its grand dimensions and also, of course, in their selection of a subdivision. Their tastes are displayed in their choice of an architectural style, or at least in the details of finish, colour, window coverings, and use of the front yard. At the same time, detachment expresses the individuality of the family, its separateness from others. The absence of shared walls reduces the number of occasions on which the lives of the family and those of its neighbours – the parties, the arguments, and the daily activities – will impinge on each other. The desire for a quieter privacy has surely been a major motive in the move to the suburbs, sometimes coupled with the desire for respectable social display.

Today, most single-family dwellings are owner-occupied, and these two aspects of suburban living may seem to be inextricably intertwined. Historically, however, this was not the case. Until the 1950s tenants outnumbered owners in most urban areas, and, except in Montreal, apartments accounted for only a small proportion of all tenant-occupied dwellings. Inevitably, then, many single-family houses were rented: the proportion exceeded 50 per cent in Toronto as late as 1941. Conversely, most renters – two-thirds of those in Hamilton in 1941, for example – lived in houses. In roughly equal measure, the remainder lived in apartment buildings, apartments over stores, or flats in converted houses. It was only during the post-war boom that the association between dwelling type and tenure became quite close. Owner-occupation, then, has been an issue in its own right.

Many families moved to the suburbs in order to be able to own their homes. Ownership carries a number of advantages. Among them, in a society such as Canada's, in which tenants have had limited legal rights, probably the most consistently important have been greater security of tenure and the opportunity to realize gains on a capital investment. After their marriage in 1912 a land surveyor and his wife, Edith McCall, paid $4,400 for a house in a 'nice quiet neighbourhood' of Winnipeg. As Edith commented in her diary, 'it is going to pay us far better than renting, and property there will go up decidedly in a year or so.' Her hopes, like the real estate market in that year, were inflated: when they sold their house fourteen years later, the McCalls made a net gain of only $350. In the interim, however, at least they were secure. In October 1919, a turbulent time, Edith noted that 'it seems as if everybody I know has had to move because the house was sold over their heads.' The motives of the McCalls were closely in accord with many who have bought a house in the suburbs: investment prospects, but above all security.

For many years, workers attached a higher priority to owning their home than did the middle classes. As a result, in the late nineteenth and early twentieth centuries, levels of ownership did not vary greatly from one occupational group to another, even though the ability to afford a house obviously varied. Workers did everything they could to acquire property, sacrificing convenience, and sometimes their children's education, in the process. In part, in an era when their skills and on-the-job power were being eroded, they were seeking to take control over their lives. More particularly, they wanted to escape the clutches and whims of the slum landlord, who was typically no better off than his tenant and so was compelled to skimp on repairs while extorting as much rent as possible. Again, it was much easier to make physical adaptations to a space that you owned. This was always an important consideration, but perhaps especially so during hard times, as Denyse Baillargeon suggests in her study of Montreal during the Great Depression. Some families may also have seen a house as an investment, but this was not their dominant motive, and, at least according to Matthew Edel and his associates, the kind of property that workers owned was more likely to decline in value than to appreciate.

Many workers were immigrants, eager to stake a claim in the New World. It is true that specific immigrant groups differed somewhat in the weight that they gave to property ownership. The Irish and, in the twentieth century, Italians have made it a top priority, while Jews have attached more significance to education. Michael Doucet and John Weaver have presented some evidence for the persistence of these differences into the post-war period in their study of housing in Hamilton. They compared the home ownership rates of different ethnic groups after 1945, a period when tens of thousands of Italians were settling in Hamilton. Taking into account age differences, they found that rates of home ownership in 1956 were between 5 and 10 percentage points higher among the Italians than among the Anglo-Celtic majority. This difference is striking, because the incomes of Italian Canadians at that time were below the local average. Owning property was an all-consuming goal for this group, as it has been, in varying degrees, for most immigrants and workers.

In contrast, for many decades the professional middle classes saw the home more as an investment, and they often found it wanting. They believed that it was preferable to rent an imposing mansion, large enough to entertain colleagues and associates and to house a servant or two, than to pay extra in order to own something smaller. However, attitudes did begin to change soon after the turn of the century. Servants became scarcer, more expensive, and more difficult to manage. As the woman of the house became responsible for its daily upkeep, tastes changed and the houses of the middle-class became smaller. In the same period, Margaret Marsh has discerned the emergence of a new style of male domesticity in which middle-class men came to express more interest in hobbies, gardening, and limited forms of do-it-yourself. Home ownership soon became almost as high a priority for professionals as for workers. In Winnipeg, for example, the McCalls were married in the midst of this shift in middle-class attitudes. In addition to buying their house, they employed a cleaning woman – a waning, if modest sign of middle-class status – even though this meant that Edith had to do prodigious amounts of canning and could not afford to buy a book for several years. On the other hand, they were careful to buy a house without any pretension: three up, three down, 'just exactly *enough* room.' By the 1920s the shift in middle-class attitudes was almost complete. The modern association of single-family residence with home ownership was well on the way to being firmly established.

The one place in Canada, and indeed in North America, where families did not consistently make home ownership a high priority until after the Second World War was Montreal. In the early decades of this century, the City of Montreal had one of the lowest rates of home ownership on the continent. For a time its rate was even lower than that of New York, where high land values kept property ownership beyond the reach of most households. Contemporaries explained Montreal's unusual situation by widespread poverty and the supposed indifference of francophones to the home ownership ideal. Marc Choko has recently challenged the latter suggestion. The evidence of local tax records shows that between 1921 and 1951 home ownership rates were consistently higher among francophones than among anglophones. The difference was not great, but it was striking, given that on average francophones had lower incomes and were less likely to live in single, detached dwellings. It is true that, among the larger suburbs, levels of owner-occupation varied with average incomes, being higher in Outremont and Westmount than in Lachine and Verdun. Within any given suburb, however, there was generally little difference between anglophones and francophones. In Outremont and Westmount, as in the city, many affluent anglophone families made a positive decision to rent, at least until the 1940s. Thereafter, home ownership rates in Montreal have risen rapidly, so that they are now approaching those in other metropolitan areas. It may be that in Montreal, among both francophones and anglophones, the goal of suburban home ownership was challenged for many years by an alternative ideal of urbanity.

If the owner-occupied, detached dwelling expresses a private life of domesticity, it can do so most fully in a situation where it is removed from the sights, sounds, smells, and symbolic associations of the workplace. Many writers have seen the residential suburb as a sylvan retreat from the bustle and corruption of working life, a place to escape to and recuperate. It functioned that way above all for men; most wives (and some servants) lived and worked there all day. This point can be overstated, since many women have always commuted. Until the Second World War, it was common for unmarried women (and men) to live with their parents while taking paid employment, often in clerical jobs. Since such jobs were usually concentrated in the downtown area, in the larger cities some young women faced quite long commutes, usually by streetcar. Then again, even during the early post-war years, when an exceptionally high proportion of married women were focusing their energies upon the domestic tasks of raising young children, a minority also went out to work. Still, residential suburbs in the first six decades of this century did embody a marked gender division of labour. Pierre Drouilly has prepared maps that show the metropolitan geography of labour force participation in Montreal in 1951 and 1961. They reveal that in the central areas of Montreal more than half the working-age women were in the labour force, while the proportion in the suburbs was typically below 30 per cent. In contrast, participation rates for men varied little between city and suburb. Residential suburbs were separated from the places of paid work; they were hives and ghettoes of unpaid labour. Embodying a gender division of labour, they expressed on a generous scale a specific domestic ideal.

In seeking residential retreats, families have wanted to avoid not only the social and symbolic associations of working life in the city but also the congested pollution with which it was usually linked. In the late nineteenth century, urban areas were decidedly unhealthy places. Mortality rates, especially for infants, were higher in urban than in rural areas. Contemporaries believed that the least healthy places were the inner-city slums, and the available evidence does indicate that suburbs were indeed healthier. In *The Anatomy of Poverty*, social historian Terry Copp reproduced a contemporary map of infant mortality rates in Montreal. His study of working-class living conditions in early twentieth-century Montreal shows that the healthiest places in the urban area were the affluent suburbs of Westmount and Outremont and the scarcely less affluent west-end wards of St Andrew and St George. The least healthy were the older working-class districts below the hill and in the near east end: St-Henri, St-Joseph, St-Gabriel, Lafontaine, Papineau, and Ste-Marie. Newer working-class suburbs, such as Maisonneuve and Delorimier, lay between these extremes. Some of the variations in infant mortality were due to differences in cultural practices. Historical geographers, including Sherry Olson, Patricia Thornton, and Michael Mercier, have suggested that francophone mothers breastfed less often and their infants paid the price. Even so, it does seem that location, as well as class and ethnicity, shaped the social incidence of health.

Of course, especially in a period of rapid population growth, most new settlement must occur at or near the urban fringe. Typically, the form that development takes does not simply reflect the tastes and preferences of prospective residents. With few exceptions, Canadian suburbs have been built by entrepreneurs and companies that sought to make a profit by producing what they could induce people to buy. In general, they have offered what their customers wanted, but when they have been in any doubt, their judgments have also been shaped by what they deemed to be most profitable. Low-density suburban development, of the sort that has become commonplace, has been especially profitable to land developers, builders, and the manufacturers of myriad goods and services, from cars to lawn care. As Edel and his associates have argued, it has been aggressively promoted by real estate entrepreneurs for well over a century. Highly leveraged forms of home ownership – down payments of less than 10 per cent and amortized repayment over twenty-five years or more – can be very profitable to lending institutions. It would be absurd to argue that the demand for mortgaged suburban living has simply been created, but it would be naïve to ignore the fact that it has also been profitably nurtured through advertising. Increasingly, as I show in chapters 5 and 6, the state has played a significant role in this area as well as developers.

A taste for suburbs has also been promoted sometimes by agencies with a social agenda, usually those that favour what we would now call 'family values.' The most striking case was Quebec between the late 1930s and the 1950s. In that period, a number of those associated with the provincial Roman Catholic church were concerned about the very high proportion of Quebeckers, especially in Montreal, who lived at high residential densities, whether in small apartment buildings or plexes. In 1940 Joseph-August Gosselin, a lawyer, and Jean-d'Auteuil Richard, a Jesuit priest, helped to form an organization, L'Union économique d'habitations (UED), that would address this issue by promoting the construction of inexpensive, owner-occupied, detached houses in new suburban subdivisions. The UED launched a model project in Montreal, Cité-Jardin du Tricentenaire, which was scheduled to open on the 300th anniversary of the city's settlement. A promotional flyer that was distributed in 1942 expressed the thinking of the union: 'La MAISON garantit la santé physique et morale de la FAMILLE. La PETITE PROPRIÉTÉ garantit le salut de la SOCIÉTÉ. L'INDUS-TRIE de BÂTIMENT garantit L'ACTIVITÉ ÉCONOMIQUE du pays' (original emphasis). In translation, its conclusion was that 'To work for the better housing of our people is to work for our families, our society, our prosperity.' This and later projects, such as the one that the Cooperative d'habitation de Montréal developed in St-Léonard, were supported by the League of Catholic Workers. In Quebec, such projects helped to foster a demand for a particular form of suburban development. Elsewhere, for the most part, such promotion was not needed.

Suburbs, then, have been promoted and settled for a variety of reasons that, collectively, express a good deal about Canadian society: a belief in the primacy of laissez-faire development, individualism, the right to property, and the virtue of private domesticity. But not everyone who speculated in suburban land made a profit; not everyone who bought a suburban house found domestic happiness or even recouped the investment. The consequences of our actions routinely escape our intentions. Indeed, the growth of suburbs has had effects that no one intended, or perhaps even desired.

The Consequences of Suburban Development

Young couples have acquired detached houses in residential suburbs because they believed they would be comfortable and secure places in which to raise children. Those who were far-sighted and who themselves had grown up in suburbs may have had a fairly complete picture of exactly what their new home environment would have to offer, although in every generation this picture has been different. More typically, new suburban residents have not been fully aware of the constraints and opportunities that they would face. The new environment has forced them to learn and adapt, individually and collectively, in ways that make it possible to speak of the unintended consequences of suburban development.

One of the main effects of suburban living has been to exaggerate the ways of life that created them. It is easy to overstate the point, as contemporaries have often been inclined to do. For example, in the early twentieth century, many observers expressed concern about a new type of dwelling: the apartment house. Apartments had been built in Europe and parts of the United States in the nineteenth century, but they did not appear in most Canadian cities until the first decade of the twentieth century. They were immediately resisted. As Richard Dennis has shown, in Toronto one of the most common arguments was that apartments discouraged family life, which was assumed to be the proper goal of all adults. Easy to clean and maintain, they encouraged women to turn away from domestic responsibilities, even childbearing. Because they contained unsupervised spaces, including entrance halls and corridors, that were neither public nor private, apartments were thought to threaten privacy and to encourage immorality.

In contrast, the individual house was believed to exert a positive influence. Augustus Bridle portrayed this influence in an evocative piece that he wrote in 1903. He takes us on an afternoon stroll in one of the better working-class districts of Toronto, a street of single-family homes. We hear an out-of-tune piano, a pedlar's call, and the bell of a scissors grinder. He shows us children coming back from the corner store with a pound of lard or a loaf of bread. And then he beckons to us, drawing our attention to a 'a real picture of contented serenity ... a young girl reading a newspaper on her doorstep.' She is smiling to herself. Why? Because, in Bridle's words, 'she loves her home better than the street.' All is right with the world, he seems to say, if children grow up in dwellings like this, where public and private spaces are kept strictly apart, where houses have front steps, and where family members have the incentive to stray no further. English-style terraced houses or the cheaper type of Montreal plexes that opened directly onto the street made such a way of life possible, but just barely. Toronto row houses, such as those he describes, or the better class of plexes with postage-stamp front yards were a slight improvement. Best of all, however, was the detached suburban house.

The detached suburban dwelling has not only sheltered the private, nuclear family, but also contributed actively to its evolution. On suburban lots detached houses are usually larger than those in the city, and size matters. Larger houses make it possible for more family members to have a room of their own, thus fostering personal privacy. At the same time, they enable the creation of new types of space that encourage families to spend more time in the home. This feature has been especially important for men and children. Depending upon their interests, and more generally on their class, many men used to spend their leisure time in the bar or at the club. Children played on the street. Since those times, suburban homes have grown to accommodate workshops and 'rec' (recreation) rooms, eventually boasting televisions and audio equipment, which have encouraged men and children to spend more time in the home or backyard.

The growth of owner-occupation has reinforced the tendency of family life to turn inwards. The effect is most dramatically apparent in those situations, rare in Canada, where large numbers of tenant families have been relocated from a 'slum' area to owner-occupied houses in a suburb. In a fascinating study set in London, England, during the 1950s, Peter Willmott and Michael Young showed that one of the more significant effects of such a relocation was a significant growth in do-it-yourself (DIY) activity. Men, especially, began to show an interest in DIY in order to save money, to build up the value of their investment, as a means of self-expression, and as a source of pride. It would be dangerous to extrapolate too freely from this study. The relocation occurred at a time when there was a boom in DIY, and in some respects the setting was unique, not only to England, but indeed to London. It is significant, however, that a later study set in Toronto reached a broadly similar conclusion. Comparing renters and owners, the sociologist William Michelson concluded not merely that owner-occupation was associated with the expenditure of time on gardening and home maintenance, but that it actually had a causal influence. The cautious conclusion that he drew from comparing his own findings with those of Wilmott, Young, and other researchers, was that suburbs did not mandate a family-centred way of life, but they fostered this as 'the path of least resistance.'

If suburbs encourage families to turn inwards it may seem that they discourage radicalism and an engagement in broad social issues. Certainly, property ownership encourages a commitment to local issues. Homeowners live in an area in which they also have a financial stake. They are likely to oppose any type of development that threatens property values, which has usually meant anything other than single-family houses. Some of the early critics of apartment buildings were motivated by moral principles, but many were local property owners, battling to defend their investment. Opposition to apartments and other even less desirable land uses typically was localized and found expression in petitions for the local municipality to exclude specific types of land use from certain areas. The exclusionary practice of zoning grew by accretion. As Peter Moore has shown in a study of Toronto, by mid-century a long series of such petitions had created a situation whereby large areas of the city were designated as residential in character, and in many of these districts apartments were prohibited. Public petitions were at first the preferred mechanism of exclusion in areas that had already seen some development. In newer, suburban districts zoning was at first accomplished privately by local developers, who recognized that prospective owners were willing to pay a premium for houses in areas that were guaranteed to contain only single-family dwellings. Home ownership, then, provides an incentive for social segregation.

Because owners must pay a good deal to sell their houses – apart from legal fees, in recent decades vendors who use real estate agents have typically paid a 5–6 per cent commission – they move much less frequently than tenants. This is another reason why homeowners care more about their area of residence and are more likely to become involved in local issues, whether pertaining to schools or to changes in land use. It is worth their while to invest the time to make local changes; faced with an unsatisfactory situation, tenants are more inclined to exit the community. Until the third quarter of this century, the municipal franchise also encouraged owners to participate in local politics. Tenants were not permitted to vote in Toronto's municipal elections until 1958, for example, and in some cities they had to wait until the 1960s. For all these reasons, homeowners have been in the vanguard of local NIMBY (not-in-my-backyard) opposition to proposed developments that are perceived to be physically or socially noxious. At the extreme, residents in fringe areas oppose *any* type of development on the grounds that it spoils the neighbourhood. Such opposition has become common in recent years, since it can now huddle under the cloak of environmental responsibility. Around Toronto, for example, opponents to further development on the Oak Ridges Moraine have emphasized the threat to Toronto's aquifer. In earlier decades, before such reasoning was understood or accepted as legitimate, it was more difficult for suburban residents to mount blanket opposition to development. Being more selective, they nevertheless found much to engage their energies. Home ownership, then, has helped to focus political energies close to home, where typically they have chosen to resist change.

The very newness of the suburbs also encouraged their first residents to become politically active. In the early post-war suburbs there was a good deal of pressure to join local associations, and the one to which almost everyone belonged was the Home and School. Occasionally these organizations existed from the beginning, being part of the developer's original conception. That was true, for example, in the Cité-Jardin du Tricentenaire and in St-Léonard, where sponsors encouraged cooperation, for example, in the establishment of a local grocery store. Those who wished to buy homes in Thorncrest Village, outside Toronto, had to apply to the Village Association. This entailed submitting a financial statement and personal data sheet, as well as passing an interview. Successful applicants were steered towards appropriate hobby and interest groups, automatically became members of the association, and so shared the responsibility of maintaining community facilities. But such carefully packaged suburbs were the exception.

In the great majority of new subdivisions, local associations had to be created, and it was usually women who led the way. Veronica Strong-Boag reports that in North Burnaby's new subdivisions it was women who established parent-teacher groups; in Don Mills they set up babysitting cooperatives; in Thornhill they formed a community kindergarten; and in North York they started a Parents Action League against sexual attacks on young children. As Harry Henderson observed in *Harper's* magazine in 1954, young parents with organizational interests and abilities had exceptional scope for their talents in the new 'mass suburbs.' In particular, in a situation where many families were moving into areas that still lacked basic services, residents' associations were formed to lobby their elected representatives. Here again, women were prominent. In Etobicoke in 1955, for example, they stormed a council meeting, protesting the failure of their developer to finish sidewalks and ditching. As Strong-Boag observes, it was the women who transformed suburbs into good neighbourhoods. We know most about such grass-roots activism in the post-war suburbs, but it surely happened just as frequently in earlier decades, when it was even more common for suburbs to grow up with few or no public services. For example, John Weaver reports that during the 1910s and 1920s ratepayers' associations formed in a number of districts in Vancouver, including Eburne, South Hastings, and Kitsilano, where they lobbied for sewers and streetcar lines.

There was much community-building to be done at the urban fringe, especially for those ethnic minorities who wished to maintain their identity. As Etan Diamond has shown, Orthodox Jews would not move into a suburb unless key community institutions had been established, including a synagogue and congregation, religious schools and youth groups, and services such as a kosher grocery store. Members of other minorities were more willing to assimilate. Like most native-born Canadians, they found that suburban living made people more community minded than they had anticipated – in some cases more than they wished. This fact, as much as anything, lay behind the complaints from contemporaries about the social pressures to join and conform during the early post-war suburban boom. Of particular interest are the comments of several of the first residents of Thorncrest Village, as reported by sociologist S.D. Clark. Families that bought a house in this subdivision knew in advance that they were entering a structured community. Even so, many were surprised at what they found. As one person commented, 'We didn't know anyone when we moved here. Our neighbours came and called on us. There was a tea for all the neighbours. We went to the next club dance. We didn't really know what to expect in a planned community. We never had much neighbourhood life before.' The difference between Thorncrest Village and most other new suburbs was not the amount of visiting that went on. From his survey of larger, generic suburbs Harry Henderson reported that in new 'communities of strangers, where everybody realizes his need for companionship, the first year is apt to witness almost frantic participation in all kinds of activities. Later, as friends are made, this tapers off somewhat.' What set Thorncrest Village apart was that the associational structure existed from the very beginning. Elsewhere, such structure had to be built from scratch. Very few of those who moved into new suburbs realized the full implications.

S.D. Clark has explored the consequences of new suburban settlement, taking his argument to a logical conclusion. He proposes that we define the suburban way of life as the process by which they are made livable. Once people have settled in, he suggests, the social life of the suburbs becomes little different from that of the city. In both places people commute, work, maintain their homes, raise children, entertain, and are entertained. What is briefly unique to the suburbs is the period of active settlement, when the country is being transformed into the city. During this short span of time, everyone gets to know their neighbours, formal and informal associations are made, and the institutions that will structure life in the new place are established. Since the majority of the people moving to the suburbs are families with young children, suburbanism is focused upon the needs of the nuclear family. The associations and institutions that must be built are, disproportionately, those associated with young children: finding playmates and babysitters, setting up sports clubs and teams, forging links with new schools, and so forth. In time the new networks and structures are established, and the social intensity of the early years wanes. The suburb and its residents begin to age. People move out and others move in. Its demographic profile becomes more similar to that of the general population. As land values rise, multi-unit dwellings are built. In a matter of years, and certainly in a decade or two, it ceases to be distinctively suburban.

Clark's argument about what happens to suburban society over time is consistent with what we know about those Canadian suburbs whose pattern of development has been traced over a period of years. In the early years of this century there was extensive cooperation among neighbours in Toronto's immigrant suburbs, as people helped each other to erect houses, community halls, and church buildings and as clergy organized settlement clubs, daycare centres, and social evenings. In a decade or so, much of this activity had dissipated. The same pattern seems to have occurred in St-Léonard after the Second World War, but strictly speaking, Clark's argument has never been tested in Canada. An Australian study, however, does bear it out. In 1966, when Lois

Bryson and Ian Winter examined a new, planned suburb of Melbourne, they found close and intense networks of socializing. A quarter of a century later they found that people had fewer friends among their immediate neighbours, who were now typically kept at a social distance. The settlement phase was over, and from Clark's point of view the place had ceased to be suburban. But surely this is too narrow a view. Clark's precise definition of 'suburban' is too much at variance with the manner in which Canadians (and Australians) have usually thought about their suburbs to be widely useful. It underlines the fact that, especially in the early years of settlement, the physical character of the suburbs shapes the lives of its residents. But it does not help us to understand whether and how such an influence might continue to define suburban needs and interests.

Many observers have supposed that, if suburban homeowners are inclined to focus on the defence of local needs and interests, they are also conservative in the broader political sense that they espouse policies that place them on the right of the political spectrum. Homeowners, after all, have at least a modicum of wealth and to that extent a stake in society. Such views were just as true in the past, when many homeowners were quite poor, as in the present. Introducing a short-lived housing program to the House of Commons in 1918, for example, Thomas Rowell elaborated upon this idea: 'It is in the national interest that a man may have opportunity to rear his family in a comfortable house of his own,' he declared. By way of explanation, he claimed that, at a time of national unrest, this 'undoubtedly induces him to take a more practical interest in the affairs of the country and thus tends to the strength and stability of our national life.' Some writers have argued that one of the reasons why socialist and social-democratic parties have been weaker in the United States and Canada than in Europe is that a significant number of North American workers have been able to acquire their own houses. They have also suggested that in countries such as Canada the long-term growth of suburban home ownership has contributed to the declining radicalism (*embourgeoisement*) of the working class. There is some truth to these sweeping claims, but they are crude and can be misleading.

Some of the more radical movements in modern Canadian history were rooted in suburban communities of working-class homeowners, especially those who had built their own homes. In the first half of the twentieth century these radical suburbs included South Vancouver, Winnipeg's North End, and both York and East York, to the northeast and northwest of Toronto, respectively. In South Vancouver and Burnaby, the socialists of the 1910s held meetings in shacks and on street corners. Arthur Evans and Ernest Winch, a carpenter, built homes there. Evans later led the On-to-Ottawa Trek during the 1930s, while Winch helped to found the Co-operative Commonwealth Federation (CCF) in 1932 and represented Burnaby for over twenty years. In 1919 the North End of Winnipeg nurtured one of the major labour confrontations in Canadian history. During the Great Depression, East York and York were home to powerful and militant associations of workers that fought for welfare relief and organized resistance against evictions. These, too, were among the earliest Ontario communities to elect CCF members, including Joseph Noseworthy and Agnes Macphail, who in 1943 became one of the first two women in the Ontario legislature. At different times, but in each place, communities of suburban homeowners showed militant radicalism. It is true that each of these communities was peopled by workers and immigrants with strong labour traditions. It is not surprising, then, that during hard times they would mobilize. Clearly, however, suburban home ownership did not inhibit their militancy and, to the extent that it was threatened by the bailiffs, it probably contributed. Pat Troy suggests that the same has also been true in Australia, but in the United States many white, working-class suburbs turned conservative when faced with the prospect of an influx of African-Americans.

Over time the character of home ownership has changed. As I describe in chapters 5 and 6, since the 1940s it has become much more common for families to acquire houses only with the assistance of extensive, insured, long-term credit. This trend has reduced the risks of buying and also strengthened the buyer's interest in maintaining the status quo. Both developments and a general rise in the standard of living have probably made owners more consistently conservative. It may be that the growth of suburban home ownership eventually helped to make Canada's workers more conservative, but if so, this influence became apparent only after the Second World War.

In the process of buying new, detached houses, families often found themselves at, and sometimes beyond, the urban fringe. Many wanted to be there to relish the sights and sounds of the country, and they enjoyed the prospect of putting the city at arm's length. Most of them realized that this would mean a degree of isolation, especially for women. The Vallières family were a case in point. In the early 1940s Vallières père worked at the Angus Repair Shops of the Canadian Pacific Railway and lived nearby in Frontenac Park, in Montreal's East End. After the war, as land speculators subdivided territory on the south shore, he was attracted to the idea of owning a house on its own plot. One weekend he took his seven-year-old son, Pierre, on a bus ride across the Jacques-Cartier bridge to view a modest property that was for sale in Longeuil-Annexe. On the way back, Pierre later recalled, his father 'was dreaming of the house he would build out of this shack he had decided to buy.' Pierre added that 'it remained only to convince my mother of the advantages of exile to the suburbs.' They were successful in this mission, and Pierre grew up as another radical son of Canada's working-class suburbs, this time as both a socialist and a *séparatiste.*

Some women did not fully realize what suburban exile might mean. As reporter Harry Henderson commented in 1954, 'city-bred women,' in particular, 'suffer greatly from

3   The home of Pierre Vallières, Longeuil, Quebec. Like thousands of other houses on Montreal's south shore after 1945 and like hundreds of thousands built in Canadian suburbs up to the 1950s, this house was owner-built and then owner-remodelled. Vallières's life story challenges the common assumption that suburbanites are conservative. (Richard Harris, 1995)

loneliness.' In recent decades feminists have argued that these early post-war suburbs were especially oppressive. They were built around the automobile and were poorly served by public transportation, if at all. Very few families had more than one car, and men usually required it to travel to work. Many women were marooned at home, often with young children and with no adult company except for neighbours who were in the same situation. The physical conditions in these post-war suburbs were generally far superior to those of Depression-era slums, but the social isolation created stresses that, in Betty Friedan's famous phrase, became 'the problem that has no name.' Friedan, like some other writers, overstated the case. Veronica Strong-Boag interviewed some of the Canadian mothers and the girls who grew up in these early post-war suburbs. She found that, looking back, most were content with the choices they had made. But they acknowledged that there was a price to living in the suburbs, one that they had not fully anticipated. Women and men chose to buy detached houses in new subdivisions at the urban fringe. They had their reasons. But once there, they found that their lives changed in more ways than they had anticipated.

3

Cities and Suburbs

Suburbs have often been seen as a 'marriage' of city and country, although 'offspring' would be a more appropriate metaphor. In physical terms they lie between their two parents and share some of the features of each. Many writers have viewed the offspring as healthier than either parent. The most influential was the English writer Ebenezer Howard, who, in *Tomorrow: A Peaceful Path to Real Reform* (1898; republished in 1902 as *Garden Cities of Tomorrow*), argued that the city offered social opportunities but divorced families from nature; that it contained good jobs but high rents, diverse amusements but slums, congestion, and polluted air. In its turn the country was beautiful and restorative, but it lacked society or much in the way of a livelihood for all but a small minority. In their stead, he argued for what he called *Garden Cities*, planned communities with a population of about 30,000, surrounded by agricultural land, on the fringe of existing urban centres. They would offer the best of the city and the country: jobs and social opportunities as well as ready access to nature.

Peter Hall has described Howard as 'the most important single character' in the history of modern urban planning, but in Canada this was not true. Garden City developments were proposed, but few were built. More influential were the ideas and plans of Howard's contemporary, the American John Olmsted. In the 1890s John took over the family

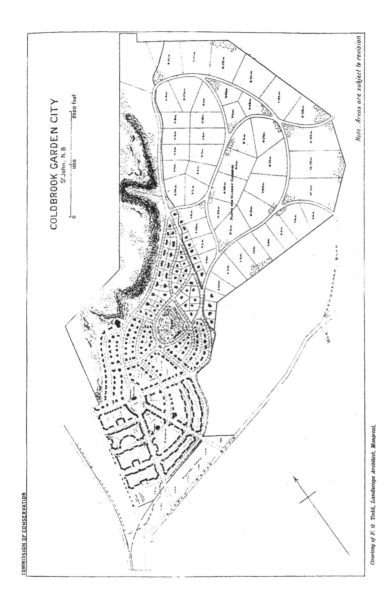

COLDBROOK GARDEN CITY
St. John, N.B

0   1000   2000 feet

Courtesy of F. G. Todd, Landscape Architect, Montreal.

Note. Areas are subject to revision

4   The plan for Coldbrook Garden City, Saint John, New Brunswick, 1913. In the early 1900s a number of land subdividers evolved schemes for self-contained suburbs with curvilinear streets and a mixture of homes and industry. Some, like Coldbrook, even made provision for municipal buildings (left centre) and garden plots (right). Few of these schemes came to fruition. (Canada. Commission of Conservation, Annual Report, 1913)

landscape design business from his grandfather, Frederick Law Olmsted. By 1907 he was laying out his first subdivision in Canada, The Uplands, in suburban Victoria, British Columbia. This established his trademark model of gracious houses and irregularly shaped lots on treed, curvilinear streets. Soon Olmsted and his apprentices and associates were in great demand. Their services were hired by the Hudson's Bay Company and the Canadian Pacific Railway (CPR), which together owned vast tracts of land around the major cities in western Canada. By the 1920s at least one example of Olmsted's planned suburban ideal existed in each of Vancouver, Edmonton, Calgary and Winnipeg. To their occupants, such suburbs seemed to be very handsome offspring indeed.

Other writers and contemporaries viewed the suburban combination of city and country in very different terms. Speaking about English suburbs, for example, F.M.L. Thompson endorses the disparaging comments published in the *Architect* in 1876: 'A modern suburb is neither one thing nor the other,' an anonymous writer commented. 'It has neither the advantages of the town nor the open freedom of the country, but manages to combine in nice equality of proportion the disadvantages of both.' The spirit of this criticism was repeated many times in Canada. In 1957 writing as the director of planning for the Hamilton-Wentworth Planning Board, Norman Pearson suggested that the uniformity of the suburbs is 'a destruction of the true benefits of the country and a negation of the qualities of the city.' Critics, then, have also seen suburbs as the issue of city and the country, although in their view misconceived.

In fact, suburbs owe very little to the country. Their very name, 'sub-urbs,' implies that they exist, function, and should be seen primarily in relation to the city. In their medieval roots suburbs lay outside the fortress city walls. On the defensive sites that were for many years typical, they literally lay below the city itself, and in social terms, too, they were lowly. Then and since, they have functioned primarily as adjuncts to the city. This is most obviously true of the purely residential, 'bedroom' communities, from which people journey to city jobs, but industrial suburbs also have been closely tied to their nearby urban centre, not only in terms of commuting but also in terms of the linkages among employers. The character of suburbs then is fundamentally urban. Residents rely on wage income from non-agricultural employment. Their daily rhythms, no less than those of the city, are governed by the clock, not the seasons. The suburbs are not the offspring of city and country but rather, in the words of Harlan Douglass, 'the city thinned out.' To make sense of the history of Canadian suburbs we need to see them above all as an aspect of the continuing process of urbanization.

The Causes and Consequences of Urbanization

Throughout most of recorded history, only a small minority of people lived in urban areas, typically between 5 and 10 per cent of the total population. This situation began to change in the eighteenth century. New agricultural technology enabled farmers to support a larger number of people in non-agricultural activity. By 1850 a census reflected the fact that Britain had become the first 'urban' nation, with more than half of its population living in cities and towns. Several European countries were not far behind, but urbanization levels remained lower in North America. Substantial cities had developed along the Atlantic seaboard and the St Lawrence River, including Halifax and Montreal, but the rate of westward settlement meant that rural populations were increasing almost as rapidly. As late as 1851 only 13 per cent of Canadians lived in cities. The pace of urbanization picked up in the latter half of the nineteenth century, particularly with the spurt of industrial development that was fostered by the National Policy in the 1880s. Still, by 1900, when 80 per cent of Britain was urban, the urban proportion in Canada was barely 35 per cent, and of these almost a third lived in places of 1,000 to 5,000 residents. Although counted in the census as urban, these centres typically serviced hinterlands of farmers, fishers, or woodsmen and were scarcely urbane in outlook.

In many ways 1901 was a turning point. The mechanization of agriculture was shifting jobs from the farm to the factory. By the 1920s the last major areas for new agricultural settlement in the Canadian west were closing off. The pace of urbanization rose again, followed by a massive wave of immigrants that increased the absolute numbers of people living in cities. Cities in central Canada doubled in size between 1900 and 1914; the population of western cities more than trebled. In the mid-1920s Canada became an urban nation, and by 1961 about 70 per cent of its population lived in urban areas, double the rate of 1901. Urbanization did not level off until the 1970s, but it was during the period between 1901 and 1961 that the rate of increase was the most rapid and consistent.

The growth of cities mattered because in Canada, as in every other country that it has affected, urbanization brought changes in social life and living conditions. The social consequences were concisely stated by the Chicago sociologist Louis Wirth in the 1930s. He argued that in urban areas, especially in the largest centres, people see each other for the most part as strangers: the definitive urban experience is that of anonymity. This state enables people to act in ways that would be difficult in more intimate settings where dense social networks enforce social norms. Freedom of action creates problems when it affects the lives of others, as it is likely to do where people live cheek by jowl. It then becomes necessary for cities to develop rules to govern social life and to establish institutions to enforce those rules. It is the stop light – first used in North America in Cleveland in 1914 at the corner of Euclid and 104th – and other rules of the road, together with zoning controls, noise, health and building by-laws, that have made cities livable.

Anonymity also fosters alienation. This is not simply a subjective feeling but a problem of social organization. To survive, a democratic society must evoke concern and responsibility for the common welfare. In metaphorical terms it must answer the question: 'Who is my neighbour?' In 1911 J.S. Woodsworth, an urban reformer and later a founding member of the CCF, pointed out that this question is nowhere posed with greater force than in the modern city, where typically we do not know our fellow city-dwellers. Woodsworth gave the example of a 'modern man' who reads in the newspaper that ten workmen were injured in an industrial accident. 'What is that to him?' Woodsworth asks. 'He hardly pauses as he sips his coffee ... Even if he owned stock in the corporation in whose factories the unfortunate workmen had been employed, it would hardly occur to him that he was even remotely responsible for their injury or death.' The problem is that 'the directors, the manager, the foreman, factory inspectors – a hundred officials come between him and the victims of the accident.' Urban anonymity dissolves our sense of brotherhood. Just as urban freedoms compel cities to develop new mechanisms of social control, anonymity encourages them to seek community.

Community is found and created in many places, and it may be rooted in an almost infinite variety of interests and commitments. It is found at work, through unions and occupational groups. It is found in clubs and associations and through support for professional sports teams, one of the more popular community-building innovations of the late-nineteenth-century city. But arguably the most significant basis of community – not just because of its intrinsic importance but also because it is almost a life's work – is the commitment to raising children. By the late 1800s Canadians had come to think of suburbs as the best places for children, whether because of the larger houses and backyards, the quieter streets, or the cleaner air. Since so many families were moving to the suburbs, they became the best places to find others who shared this commitment. If suburban families have sometimes turned their backs on wider social responsibilities, they have also pursued their own search for community, one that is certainly urban in its self-consciousness.

While urbanization eroded feelings of collective kinship, it increased the social need. Urban growth, particularly in the larger industrial cities, produced a deterioration in living conditions. As cities grew, the demand for land pushed prices ever higher. To cover the cost of housing, landlords subdivided houses that had once been occupied by the middle classes, or developers replaced them with apartments and tenements. In terms of persons per room and dwellings per acre, crowding increased. The situation in Montreal was the worst in Canada and probably one of the worst on the continent. Gilliland and Olson suggest that in 1860 about 75 per cent of all Montreal households contained more than one person per room, a modern measure of overcrowding. Virtually all French-Canadians and workers would have been crowded. By the time that urban reformers had begun to concern themselves with this issue in the late 1890s, the overcrowding rate had fallen to about 40 per cent. As Peter Baskerville has shown, overcrowding was still a problem for workers and French Canadians, both within and beyond Montreal. As cities grew, however, the importance of crowding was eclipsed by the availability and quality of public services.

Crowding and inadequate services threatened the physical health of city residents, especially where garbage disposal was ineffective and where many families still relied on outdoor privies and drank polluted water. Health conditions began to improve in the 1910s, although airborne pollution from industrial sources grew worse, since it was unregulated and industrial growth was proceeding apace. The demand for regulation was weak, because factory smoke was associated with prosperity. In 1912 an advertisement for a workers' subdivision in Toronto used billowing smoke as a framing motif, coupled with the written message that settlers would have their choice of jobs. In other respects, however, air and water pollution declined. In the 1890s horse cars were replaced by electric streetcars. By the 1910s horse-drawn carriages and carts were being rapidly replaced by automobiles and trucks, which increased chemical emissions but reduced significantly the amount of manure on the streets. Public health initiatives were made in this decade in many cities. As both Michael Piva and Terry Copp have described, they included Toronto and Montreal. In Ontario the appointment in 1910 of John W.S. McCullough and Charles Hastings as the provincial and Toronto medical health officers, respectively, was an important development. The Toronto Board of Health doubled its expenditures overnight and, following passage of the Ontario Milk Act in 1911, began closely to inspect milk supplies, a common source of illness for children. By 1914 pasteurization was mandatory. Sanitation was improved. Toronto compelled property owners to install piped water and sewerage, thereby eliminating more than 10,000 privies. Education campaigns raised awareness that cities could be made more healthy. In 1912 the Toronto Board of Health established the Division of Child Welfare, and two years later the province established the Child Hygiene Bureau. Education was an important part of the mandate of both bodies. The chlorination of water and vaccination campaigns reduced the incidence of the main killer diseases, including cholera, smallpox, diphtheria, and intestinal infections. Similar steps were taken later in other cities across the country, a little later in Montreal, and latest of all in the francophone districts of that city.

Because of such initiatives, it was in the 1910s that, after rising in the late nineteenth century, infant mortality rates began to decline. In Ontario in the 1900s about 120 babies in every thousand died in their first year. In general, the situation was worst in the larger cities, especially Montreal, where in the first decade of the century more than one in four infants died. By the early 1920s the rate in Montreal had fallen to about 160 per thousand, and a similar decline had occurred throughout Ontario, but it was not until this decade that urban mortality rates fell to the same level as that of rural areas. Thus, for the first quarter of the twentieth century Canadian cities were very unhealthy places. In its various forms, crowding – sometimes subsumed under the related term 'congestion' – was generally blamed for this situation.

A particular type of crowding, that which occurred within the household, was thought to pose a moral as well as physical threat to Canadian families. In order to make ends meet, many families took in lodgers. A large survey in the United States showed that in 1903 one-quarter of all urban families contained at least one lodger or lodging family, and, for a variety of reasons that I have discussed elsewhere, the proportion in Canada was almost certainly higher. The wave of immigration of the 1900s resulted in a severe housing shortage, and the incidence of lodging increased steadily to about 1914. It fell during and after the First World War, but as late as 1931 one-quarter of all households in Canadian cities contained lodgers. In some cases, the guests were members of extended families, or, as was common in immigrant communities, they were friends and acquaintances from the old country. Quite commonly they were what Peter Baskerville has described as 'familiar strangers': people who belonged to the same occupational, linguistic, or religious communities as their hosts. They were strangers, nonetheless, and many social observers worried that bringing such people into the family posed all sorts of moral risks, especially to girls. This view was probably shared by those who took in lodgers. In a study of Toronto and Hamilton it was found that, over the first half of the twentieth century, the nature of the relationship between lodger and host became more distant. At the turn of the century almost three-quarters of all lodgers boarded, that is, they received meals and sometimes other services. By 1950 the great majority were classified in the city directory as 'roomers,' indicating that they paid only for accommodation. The steady growth of rooming, at the expense of boarding, probably suited guests as much as hosts, but either way it speaks to a growing desire for privacy. Taking in lodgers was something that people did because they had to; it was another of the undesirable consequences of city life.

Around the turn of the century the crowding, high rates of mortality, and poor housing conditions gave rise to a wide-ranging movement for urban reform. Reformers focused on housing and public health, as well as changing civic government in ways that would make it more efficient and accountable. Their historians, including Paul Rutherford and John Weaver, have disagreed about the reformers' motives, which were clearly mixed. Some, evidently, were driven by altruism. Others recognized that a city where poor living conditions fostered disease and ill-health was a poor place to do business. In a number of studies writers have attempted to sketch the dimensions of urban problems, usually by focusing upon conditions in some of the worst districts. In Montreal Herbert Ames, a businessman and philanthropist, wrote *The City below the Hill* (1897), about conditions in an older working-class district at the foot of Mount Royal. In *My Neighbor* (1911), J.S. Woodsworth drew on his observations in Winnipeg as well as upon reports from other cities, in order to portray the conditions and difficulties faced by the urban poor. In Toronto in 1917 the Bureau of Municipal Research, a reform organization, prepared a report on The Ward, an area of (mainly Jewish) immigrant settlement close to the city's core. In each case these studies concluded with a call for action. The public health and sanitary reforms that gathered momentum in the 1910s were the most significant result. Efforts were also made to improve housing conditions, although with limited effect. Toronto was one of the cities where some action was taken with regard to housing. A group of philanthropists led by Frank Beer established the

Toronto Housing Company, which built two housing projects in the city's east end to try to relieve pressure on the housing stock. Containing several hundred units, these projects were well built and well appointed. Although they eased the housing shortage, rents were too high to effectively help the poor. Elsewhere, for all the rhetoric, little was accomplished.

Conditions in Canadian cities were not generally as bad as reformers claimed. Observers were very selective in their use of examples and in many cases drew upon studies of British or U.S. cities. Critics downplayed or ignored the positive forces that existed even in the worst inner-city districts, notably the complex web of mutual assistance that residents had developed. The concepts with which we attempt to describe or grasp the social world rarely correspond exactly to reality. They are abstractions. As Alan Mayne has shown, however, in reform discourse 'slum' became at least as much a rhetorical device as it was a descriptor. If we want to know what conditions were like we would need to probe and dig behind this rhetoric. For contemporaries, however, the discourse had its own significance. Reformers believed that slums, as they described them, really existed. So, too, did many of those whom they influenced. As both reality and myth, slums became part of the argument in favour of suburbs.

Decentralization: Jobs and Transportation

As conditions in cities deteriorated up to the early years of the twentieth century, an increasing number of observers came to the conclusion that the best hope for improvement lay in the decentralization of urban areas. If transit were improved and cheapened, more people would be able to move to the suburbs. Better still, if companies created jobs in the suburbs, workers could follow. In either case, crowding and congestion at the centre would be reduced, more people would have access to cheaper suburban housing, living conditions would improve, and employees would be healthier and more productive. Everyone could gain. Reforming the city was necessary, but decentralization of houses and industry was the best hope for the future.

If a growing number of people believed that decentralization was desirable, two developments in combination made it increasingly possible. The first was the continuing decentralization of industry. Lacking historical perspective, some writers have suggested that it is only since the Second World War that significant numbers of factory jobs have been created at, or beyond, the urban fringe. In fact, as Robert Lewis has shown, such dispersion has been a feature of Canadian (and U.S.) cities since at least the mid-nineteenth century. This pattern has long been disguised by the fact that early suburban industrial districts often were soon annexed by the city. Most Canadian cities first developed as entrepots, whether on the ocean (Halifax, Vancouver), a river (Montreal), or a lake (Toronto, Hamilton). In the prairies, they depended at first on the railway. Industrial, warehousing, and office employment grew up around the transit facilities: the port or the station and freight yards.

As cities grew, many companies soon found it advantageous to relocate away from these central locations. When their operations expanded, some were able to grow in situ by acquiring adjacent sites. In this manner Massey-Harris, the leading manufacturer of farm implements in Canada for much of the twentieth century, was able to extend its plant along King Street in Toronto's inner west end. But such development was unusual. Most firms found it difficult to acquire sufficient land beside their existing facilities and so were compelled to move to the fringe. Enforced relocation became especially common after the turn of the century, when the adoption of assembly-line technology forced companies to build single-storey factories that required relatively large tracts of land. Some writers have suggested that growing labour militancy after 1900 also gave employers a nudge, prompting them to seek a more

pliable suburban labour force. There is not much evidence
that this was a significant consideration, although a survey
undertaken by G.H. Ferguson in the early 1920s did find
that Toronto companies that had recently relocated to the
suburbs enjoyed a labour advantage. In half of these companies labour turnover had declined, while in only 8 per
cent had it increased. Ferguson did not report whether
declining turnover meant that workers were happier, or
whether by living in the suburbs their alternatives were
more limited. In either case, employers benefited.

In many instances decentralization depended upon or
was encouraged by the actions of suburban governments
and land developers. By offering tax reductions, temporary
tax holidays, or other financial incentives, suburban governments sought to attract employers. This made fiscal
sense, since most companies would eventually generate
more in tax revenues than they would demand in services,
and once companies had been set up, it was likely that the
developers and builders of housing would soon follow. In
conjunction with land developers, some suburban governments accommodated planned industrial districts that
offered all necessary public services. Transportation, of
course, was a necessity, and these districts invariably
boasted waterfront access, railway facilities, or both. As
Paul-André Linteau has shown, an excellent example was
the town of Maisonneuve, which was developed after 1883
in Montreal's East End. Planned and promoted by wealthy
developers and industrialists, Maisonneuve was bordered
by the St Lawrence River east of Montreal and also was
served by the Canadian Northern Railway. The increasing
importance of the railway made it possible for industrial
districts to develop on suburban sites away from the water.
Companies that received or dispatched shipments by rail
could follow radial lines out to the city's edge in any direction. There, railway companies could capitalize on the
latent demand for freight yards by building belt lines that
circled the city.

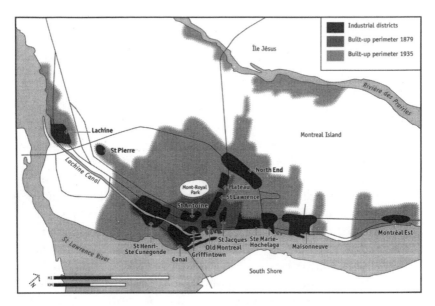

5   Manufacturing districts in Montreal, 1935. In Montreal, as elsewhere, the decentralization of factories since the mid-nineteenth century had enabled successive generations of workers to move to the suburban fringe, especially in east Montreal. (Courtesy of Robert Lewis)

Industrial suburbs that depended upon rail transportation grew up in every city. Many, for example, West Toronto Junction and the Elmwood district of Winnipeg, grew haphazardly. Others were in varying degrees planned, although this did not necessarily mean that they were more successful. New Toronto, in southern Etobicoke, was laid out in the 1880s, but it was only after the Goodyear Tire and Rubber Company built a rubber plant there in 1917 that it really began to thrive. Transcona, outside Winnipeg, was laid out just before the First World War by the Grand Trunk Pacific and Transcontinental railways, which built repair shops and freight yards. The economic boom ended in 1913, however, and the subsequent slow growth precipitated the town's bankrupcy in 1921. A more successful local project in Manitoba was the construction of the stockyards in St-Boniface. Opening for business at an inauspicious time in 1914, they soon attracted the major meat packers and so anchored later growth.

When industry moved out to the suburbs, workers almost inevitably followed. It was in everyone's interest. Employers were keen to have access to a nearby labour force, and workers were pleased to be able to acquire relatively cheap houses close to their jobs. In any case, the middle class and the social elite usually were not interested in settling in suburban areas that were shadowed by factory smoke. Leaside, a town just outside Toronto that was planned by the Canadian Northern Railway in 1912, was the exception. Here, the company laid out a garden suburb of curvilinear streets, attractive houses, and quite generous lots not far from their repair shops and an industrial district that soon contained the Durant automobile factory and the Canada Wire and Cable Company. A small workers' district, arranged on a gridiron street plan, acted as a buffer. It was too small to house many local workers, and for a while Canadian Northern had to run a special train to bring city workers out to their suburban workplaces. When they could do so, however, workers followed their employers into the suburbs. After the Goodyear plant was built in New Toronto in 1917, the company tapped the small local labour pool and drew others out. In the 1920s almost all of its workers lived nearby, many within easy walking distance. Similarly, when in the same year the Kodak Company moved a factory and its Canadian head office from a fairly central location in Toronto out to Mount Dennis in the northwestern fringe, workers followed. Before the move, although some workers commuted several kilometres, most clustered in the downtown area close by. Soon after the move, Kodak's labour shed had become decidedly suburban, many employees living in Mount Dennis or adjacent parts of York Township.

In aggregate, the decentralization of industry helped to

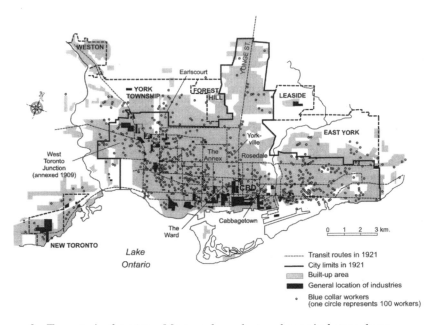

6   Toronto in the 1920s. Most workers clustered near industry: down-town, in the industrial suburb of the Junction, and in the industrial satellite of New Toronto. Many also settled in unregulated fringe districts in York and East York, where they built their own houses. (Richard Harris)

shape the evolving social geography of the urban area. The most influential model of urban structure in North America was developed by Ernest W. Burgess, a sociologist who taught at the University of Chicago in the interwar years. According to Burgess's model, which was based on his observations of Chicago, factories ringed the Central Business District (CBD) and workers clustered in rings of settlement nearby. In fact, however, the decentralization of jobs helped to create many workers' suburbs. In Toronto, workers' suburbs developed in York Township, close to the industrial district of the Junction, and in New Toronto. In Montreal, workers settled in a succession of new suburban industrial districts that developed from the late nineteenth century onward: Lachine to the west, Maisonneuve and Montréal-Est to the east, and Mile End to the north. In Hamilton, the steady expansion of steel mills, metal fabricating plants, and chemical factories along the rail lines that paralleled the southern shore of Lake Ontario drew workers in their wake, creating an expanding east end that extended into suburban Barton and then Saltfleet townships. In Winnipeg, the Point Douglas district and nearby freight yards gave employment to the diverse immigrant workers who settled the North End, while smaller clusters of industry in suburban Elmwood, Transcona, and East Kildonan also attracted settlement. In every city, suburban industry meant working-class, and often immigrant, suburbs.

If the changing geography of employment shaped Canadian suburbs in the early decades of this century, new methods of transportation were almost as important. Until the 1890s there were no effective means of mass transportation in Canadian cities. Horse cars were slow and too expensive for the great majority of workers. In Britain, national legislation had compelled railway companies to provide a train service that was cheap enough to be used by many hundreds of thousands of workers. Especially in London, this service had a significant effect in opening up new suburbs. In Canada there was no such legislation. Despite some promotional efforts, railways were little used, even by the middle class, for commuting purposes. An interesting, because failed, attempt to promote commuter traffic was the foundation of the Town of Mount Royal. In the years immediately before the First World War, the Canadian Northern Railway was eager to obtain access to central Montreal. In order to do so, however, it would have to build a costly, three-mile tunnel. To fund this project, the proprietors conceived the scheme of laying out a model community on the other side of the tunnel. Profits from land development and revenues from local commuter traffic were supposed to pay their costs. To this end, land development in Mount Royal was begun in 1912. As with

Transcona, however, the timing was bad. The town was settled very slowly through the interwar years and never generated much commuter rail business. By the time that it was fully built up in the 1950s, most residents had cars.

Given that railways were infrequently used for commuting, the introduction of the electric streetcar in the 1890s soon had a substantial impact. By the time that urban growth resumed and gathered pace in the 1900s, streetcars had become affordable to a significant number of urban workers. In this era, Canadian cities were quite compact, and by American or British standards most were relatively small. It was feasible for many families to settle in the suburbs and, if necessary, for the wage earner to commute all the way downtown by streetcar. For many years, transit service was provided by companies that held a local monopoly. In the United States, these companies typically built lines into virgin territory, anticipating and leading growth. Viewed narrowly, this approach made no sense; it meant that companies had to make large investments years before they earned equivalent revenues. As Sam Bass Warner has shown, however, their directors also owned and speculated in suburban land. They treated streetcar lines as loss leaders for land development. Here, it is possible to speak of streetcar suburbs, whose extent and form was shaped by this linear technology. To some extent the same overlap of business interests occurred in Canada. Ottawa provides a nice example, which has been documented by Bruce Elliott in his history of suburban Nepean. In 1893, soon after the Ottawa Electric Railway was established by Thomas Ahearn and Warren Soper, the residents of Hintonburg, a small settlement to the west of Ottawa, incorporated themselves as a village, so that they would be able to sign an agreement with the railway company to provide service. The Electric Railway was very willing to oblige. In 1892 Ahearn and Soper had joined with other business associates to form the Ottawa Land Association, which had immediately bought farms in Hintonburg. Straddling the line that the Electric

Railway company soon built along Holland Avenue, in 1895 these farms were subdivided into building lots and eventually sold at a tidy profit.

With or without such corporate connections, in the early years it was common for the developers of exclusive suburbs to arrange for streetcar service. One of John Olmsted's first thoughts during the early planning of The Uplands was to enquire whether the local streetcar company would be willing to extend its service into the area. Similar concerns guided lobbying activity in Vancouver's Shaughnessy Heights, where development began in 1907–8, and in Winnipeg's Tuxedo Park (1904–5). Before automobiles became reliable, the social elite had demanded the convenience of the streetcar. This phase, however, was short lived. By 1911 the Dovercourt Land, Building and Savings Company was promoting Lawrence Park in North Toronto, chiefly through advertisements in *Canadian Motorist*. Streetcars always meant mass transportation, and for those who could afford something better they were seen as a drawback.

In more modest suburbs, some developers were also able to arrange for the provision of transit service. This was common in western Canada. In Edmonton, as Peter Smith has shown rather elegantly in a plate that he prepared for *The Historical Atlas of Canada*, streetcar lines serviced fringe areas of settlement to the northeast, northwest, and southeast and led it to the west and southwest. They also helped to provoke speculation in far-flung lots in the years leading up to the First World War. In Winnipeg, the promise of streetcar service was integral to the promotion of Transcona, although when this project faltered, the half-laid tracks were torn up. More usefully, streetcar service promoted the growth of Elmwood. Some development had occurred in this area before the turn of the century, but it accelerated in 1903 when a new line across the Louise Bridge connected the area with jobs in Point Douglas. In western cities, then, streetcars led and shaped suburban development.

7   Aerial view of west Edmonton, 1924. Spines and doglegs of suburban development had grown up along streetcar lines. Along curvilinear streets Glenora, soon to become the city's elite suburb, was taking shape (left centre). Extensive land in the northeast was being held in reserve by the Hudson's Bay Company. (National Air Photo Library. C.19.74.12)

In the cities of eastern and central Canada, however, the streetcar companies were more cautious. In some instances they kept pace with new fringe development. In Montreal, for example, streetcar service boosted development in young Verdun after 1899 and was vital to the early prosperity of Maisonneuve. Elsewhere it lagged. In Hamilton, for instance, streetcar lines were always a few years behind the workers who were settling the east end. Occasionally, streetcar companies made little or no attempt at all to service the suburbs. An extreme case occurred in Toronto, where in 1891 the Toronto Railway Company (TRC) had been given a thirty-year exclusive franchise to provide street rail service to the city. During the 1900s the City of Toronto had expanded by annexing a number of suburbs, and population growth pushed the built-up area beyond even these new city limits into suburban York Township. But the TRC refused to extend its lines beyond the city limits as they had existed in 1891. By the 1910s, in desperation, the city built some short feeder lines in the newly annexed districts. Even so, suburbs grew up beyond the streetcar lines in every direction. Many of those who made their home in these unserviced suburbs did use the streetcar to travel to work, but in order to do so they had to walk a kilometre or two to reach the end of the line. Indirectly, these suburbs were shaped by the streetcar. Since they were not generally attractive to the middle classes, they were settled largely by workers, many of whom were recent immigrants from Britain who were willing to put up with inconveniences in order to acquire a house. At least in central and eastern Canadian cities, however, streetcars had a more restrained impact on suburban development than they did in the United States or western Canada.

As a means of mass transportation, the electric streetcar was a huge advance. It was cheap, potentially fast, and pollution free. But it was far from ideal. Streetcars could not manoeuvre around obstacles and often ground to a halt on congested roads. Metal wheels ran on metal rails, and the early models were extraordinarily noisy. Frequently they drowned out all efforts at conversation. More seriously, they provided poor air quality, especially in winter. Between 1910 and 1930 the per capita consumption of cigarettes in Canada increased five times, and when windows were closed, transit riders were breathing in a toxic fog. The solution was to ban smoking, but at a time when the health risks were unknown, such action risked alienating a growing body of riders. By 1945 twenty-one of twenty-three transit systems in Canada had instituted smoking bans, but in most cases they had done so only quite recently and probably because during the Second World War many more women were riding and working on the streetcars. Women were much less likely to smoke than men, and they found the experience of riding less to their liking. In particular, there was always the possibility of harassment – what contemporaries might have referred to as attracting unwelcome attention. This probably became more of an issue over time; after transit systems switched their vehicles to one-person operation in the 1910s, there was no longer a ticket collector to provide minimal supervision. As a result, Donald Davis, the leading historian of public transit in Canadian cities, has reported that 'sexual harassment was a continual complaint' on streetcars (and buses) before 1950.

Streetcars and, from the 1920s, buses brought people closer to their urban neighbours than many wished. They compelled riders to face people who differed not only in their smoking habits and their sex, but also in their ethnicity and class. Significantly, J.S. Woodsworth used the streetcar to illustrate his argument about the interdependence of city-dwellers. He tells how he remained on a streetcar as it travelled through a 'slum district,' the business section, and on into a 'beautiful residential suburb.' At first a 'poor wreck of a man' sat opposite him, his 'clothes dirty and foul-smelling and probably filled with vermin and disease.' The man got off, and within a few blocks the streetcar 'filled with ladies returning from their shopping expeditions.' The man's seat was now filled by 'a fashionably dressed woman,' who would have 'shrunk in disgust and fear' from the previous occupant. Woodsworth uses this example to illustrate the point that 'for good or ill' we are all members of urban society. The jitney operator, and in a few years the automobile manufacturer, might have used the story even more effectively to dramatize the limitations of public transit. In an era when people were seeking greater privacy at home, they were likely to tolerate enforced public intimacy no longer than they had to.

By the end of the First World War, the emerging alternative was the automobile. At first automobiles, like streetcars, had less effect on suburban growth in Canada than in the United States. During the minor building boom of the mid and late 1920s, very few Canadian subdivisions were developed on the assumption that residents would use cars to commute downtown. This was even true of some of the more exclusive suburbs, such as Kingsway Park in Etobicoke. This area, which was laid out just before the First World War, grew slowly but steadily during the interwar period. For years it lacked a number of services, and residents had to travel outside the area to do their banking and even to buy groceries. There was no public transit, and evidently many families did not have a car, because during the 1920s the developer found it advisable to run a private bus service along the Kingsway to the streetcar loop at Jane and Bloor streets. By the end of the 1920s, however, the developers of affluent subdivisions were catering to the automobile. Perhaps the most striking example was the development of the British Properties in West Vancouver, which was targeted at the sort of families who would otherwise have looked for houses in Shaughnessy or the better parts of Point Grey. The developer, the Anglo-Irish Guinness family, recognized that in order to attract business they would have to improve access to downtown Vancouver. With deep pockets, vision, and chutzpah, in 1938 they built the Lions Gate Bridge. In time buses were to cross the bridge, but it was auto access that they had most clearly in mind.

The more usual arrangement was for taxpayers to subsidize the car. Early automobiles were poor at negotiating muddy streets, and municipalities came under pressure to pave and improve roadways. Cars travelled faster than carts and carriages, and, as traffic increased during the 1910s, a growing number of signs, lights, and traffic police were required to regulate intersections. By the 1920s, to eliminate the jogs and bottlenecks that were holding up traffic movement, municipalities widened and straightened streets. Some new radial routes were designed primarily for cars, making new suburbs more attractive and older suburbs less so. As early as 1916 the completion of the Toronto-Hamilton highway helped to separate the leafy suburb of Parkdale from Lake Ontario, one of its main attractions. After 1945 limited-access highways carried this process to a logical conclusion. The completion of Toronto's Gardiner Expressway in 1958, for example, helped to open up the western suburbs to rapid settlement while effectively cutting off Parkdale and other residential districts from the lake. Eventually, in the late 1960s citizen opposition stopped some highway projects. Until then, however, the consensus was that subsidizing the automobile was the necessary price of progress and personal freedom.

Automobiles did not have much impact on suburban development in Canada before the Second World War. During the early 1920s the rate of automobile ownership in this country was barely two-thirds of that in the United States. Long-distance commuting and even shorter commutes that cut across the radial patterns of mass transit were rare. In a study of Kitchener and Waterloo, Ontario, it was found that in 1897 almost no workers commuted between these two neighbouring communities, even though they were geographically very close. Strikingly, much the same was true thirty years later, even though the two towns were now joined by continuous urban development. Those who worked in each community also lived there. Similarly in Toronto, those who worked in suburban areas such as New Toronto, Mount Dennis, and Leaside also tended to live nearby or close to streetcar lines that could easily deliver them to work. The great majority of people simply could not afford a car.

For a short time, the jitney saved commuters from the discomfort of the streetcar and the expense of the automobile. Jitneys were a cross between taxis and buses: they were customized automobiles that ran on fixed routes and usually charged a flat rate, picking up riders wherever they were hailed. They became popular in the early 1910s and reached their zenith in the middle of this decade, when perhaps 700 were in operation in each of Toronto and Winnipeg and almost as many in Hamilton and Vancouver. Their appeal was obvious, especially in cities where streetcar service was poor. They were about 50 per cent faster, somewhat more private, and also more convenient than streetcars. They were sometimes cramped, since jitney operators had an incentive to squeeze in as many paying customers as possible, but at least they offered everyone a seat. In contrast, a Toronto transit survey in 1915 showed that in peak hours more than two-fifths of all streetcar passengers had to stand. By the early 1920s, however, jitneys increasingly were being regulated. Their operators naturally chose to run them on the most travelled routes. Street railways complained that this practice of so-called cherry-picking was unfair competition. At one point the manager of the Vancouver street railway estimated that jitneys were costing his company 20–40 per cent of its business. The streetcar companies eventually were successful in having them banned. Donald Davis has argued that this ban was misguided, that jitneys were complementary to streetcars, and that if permitted to operate longer, they could have provided a serious alternative to the private automobile. Despite their brief moment of glory in the mid-1910s, however, they remain a fine historical example of a path not taken.

Between 1900 and 1939 the geography of Canadian cities and suburbs was shaped jointly by the decentralization of industry and the elaboration of public transit, above all, the streetcar. The combined influence of jobs and transportation could be illustrated by any of the cities that have already been mentioned in this chapter. Among those that have not Calgary was one of the most important and also one of the most rapidly growing. Max Foran has traced the changing geography of the city from its origins up to the Second World War. He has shown how land promoters attracted stockyards, abattoirs, and a brewery to East Calgary, a fringe area whose character was sealed by the subsequent construction of Canadian Pacific Railway (CPR) lines. Thereafter, manufacturing followed rail lines and drew workers into suburban districts such as Manchester and Bonnybrook. Differentiated residential areas developed rapidly as the city boomed between 1909 and 1912. Streetcars led development into a range of subdivisions, from the exclusive, CPR-owned Mount Royal, through Tuxedo Park, Pleasant Heights, Shaganappi, Killarney, and Elbow Park, down to Bowness and Forest Lawn. The geographical particularities were unique, but the main processes that were at work in Calgary were those that shaped other cities and suburbs across the country.

The Suburban Trend

The decentralization of industry and better transportation helped to make suburbs more obviously different from the city. In contrast to the overcrowded city, they allowed people to live at lower densities. Then, too, the very rapidity with which urban areas grew after 1900 meant that the new suburbs would be extensive. But the development that underlined the significance of these changes was the new reluctance of cities to annex.

Until about the First World War, cities had been eager to annex fringe territory soon after it began to be developed. Annexation was sometimes justified on grounds of efficiency in service provision, but the real reason usually was civic pride. Cities competed for business and prestige, and population counts were their currency. Affluent suburbs were not always eager to be annexed, since this meant a loss of local control and a threat to their exclusive character, but they acquiesced. Attitudes of civic boosterism and aggressive annexations persisted in the west into the early twentieth century. In the era of unbridled optimism before 1913 Calgary and Edmonton absorbed huge areas, including tracts that were not developed until after 1945. As late as 1929 Vancouver doubled in size by embracing Point Grey and South Vancouver. By then, however, in eastern cities attitudes had hardened. Toronto had annexed extensively between 1900 and 1912. The social character of these recent suburbs varied, but many lacked even basic services, such as piped water and sewers. Committed to providing this infrastructure, the city took on large debts. By 1912, when Leaside petitioned for annexation, Toronto's newly cautious council refused. Subsequent requests, notably those from York Township and East York in the late 1920s, were also rejected. Toronto undertook no more major annexations until the mid-1960s. Other cities in central and eastern Canada were less obdurate. Hamilton, notably, took in portions of surrounding Barton Township more or less in step with development. But in general a new pattern had been set.

While fiscal considerations made cities cautious about annexation, suburbs also became less enthusiastic. The residents of low-income suburbs had mixed feelings about annexation; for it meant not only an increase in services but also in taxes, which they could ill afford. The residents of affluent suburbs were more determined to maintain their identity. In the Montreal area, Westmount and Outremont evolved the strong social and civic identity that in the fall of 2000 fuelled outrage at the proposed creation of a single city government for everyone on the island. Nascent elite suburbs became proactive. Recognizing that the City of Toronto was no longer interested in annexation, in 1924 residents of the only affluent part of York Township incorporated as the Village of Forest Hill. To the west, the villagers of Swansea soon followed suit. Canadian urban areas did not experience the proliferation of suburbs that their U.S. counterparts did, but after 1900 municipal governments multiplied as suburbs diversified and cities stopped annexing.

The growth of suburbs became most obvious after about

1910. In the first decade of the twentieth century, central cities grew more rapidly (by 54 per cent) than the remainder of urban areas (35 per cent). Much of this growth was made possible by annexation. In the following decade, as annexation slowed, these percentages were reversed. Thereafter, suburbs continued to grow more rapidly than cities up to and beyond the Second World War. Between 1951 and 1961 the population of cities rose by barely 20 per cent, while that of their suburbs more than doubled. Of course, as we saw in the previous chapter, municipal status alone should not determine whether we describe an area as suburban. In the 1950s the cities of Calgary and Edmonton contained many new subdivisions that were, in effect, suburban. However, especially in the first half of the century, it did matter whether new subdivisions took shape within or beyond city limits and, if beyond, under what manner of government. To understand why, we must turn to the diverse ways in which suburbs were actually built.

4

The Making of Suburban Diversity, 1900–1929

In the first half of the twentieth century, Canadian suburbs were collectively diverse but individually homogeneous. This was a new phenomenon. In the nineteenth century, when the main function of Canadian cities was to facilitate trade, the segregation of people and land uses occurred on only a very limited scale. Ian Davey and Michael Doucet have shown, for example, that mid-nineteenth-century Hamilton did contain a distinct commercial core, but that in the residential areas merchants, professionals, and labourers often lived in the same areas and on the same city blocks. As urban industry became more important in the late nineteenth century, factories and workers' housing developed side by side. In some cases factory owners lived nearby, helping to create districts that were defined by an industry or occupation. By the early twentieth century a tanning and footwear district had developed in Quebec City, between the escarpment and the Saint Charles River. On a larger scale, in Toronto a garment district emerged immediately to the west of the downtown. In the latter case, factories, home workshops, workers' housing, merchants, and small-scale industrialists were crammed together in a way that expressed their close interdependence. Some intermingling carried over into early industrial suburbs, such as West Toronto Junction. Suburban industries established de facto occupational districts at the fringe. Many machinists settled in the residential areas around the Angus Repair Shops of the Canadian Pacific Railway (CPR) in Montreal's East End, as did rubber workers around the Goodyear plant in New Toronto. In this manner, elements of the geography of the early industrial city persisted into the twentieth-century suburb.

Especially after 1900, however, the more extensive growth of suburbs made possible the emergence of a larger-scale segregation, of industry from homes, and of rich from poor. There were suburbs devoted almost wholly to industry and others occupied exclusively by low-income workers or the social elite. Managers at Goodyear or at the CPR's Angus shops did not live close to their workplace. If Canadian suburbs of the early twentieth century embodied a thinning out of the city, this dilution permitted a re-crystallization of the main elements of urban society on a new, larger scale.

The sorting out of people and land uses yielded a collective diversity that was produced in a variety of ways. Not all suburbs were created in the same manner. In the nineteenth century, land development at the urban fringe usually occurred on a small scale. Those responsible for subdividing land usually were not involved in its subsequent development. The process was fragmented. By the 1960s, land development in most metropolitan areas was dominated by large developers that controlled all stages of the development process, from land subdivision, through home building, to marketing and even finance. As this system emerged, through the early decades of the twentieth century land development occurred in a variety of ways and produced a variety of suburbs. After discussing the segregated character of the emerging urban region of 1900–29, in this chapter I identify the ways in which suburban areas were developed and sketch the diverse results.

The Segregated Urban Region

In recent years, social observers have often expressed concern about the growing disparities between city poverty and suburban affluence. This view is especially common in the United States, where the decline of some inner cities has been very dramatic, but in many Canadian cities the city-suburban divide also has been seen as important. To a limited extent a similar contrast was implied in the early twentieth century by those reformers who dwelt upon the appalling conditions in inner city slums. In Britain and the United States, writers often contrasted the suburbs with the slums, seeing one as the solution to the other. Writers in Canada were influenced by this way of thinking, but they were also compelled to acknowledge local facts. Canada's urban poor lived in inner city slums and also in suburban shacktowns. When Thomas Adams, town planning adviser to the federal government for much of the 1910s, prepared a survey of housing conditions he commented: 'some of the worst conditions are ... just outside the boundaries of cities, where there are no sewers and no water supply.' At the same time, the social elite were at least as likely to live in city mansions as in gracious suburbs. It is true that, as suburbs acquired a reputation for being good places to raise children, they varied more from the city in terms of their demographic composition. Judging from the research of the American social historian John Modell, however, this was a shift that became striking only after the Second World War. In the earlier years of the century, the most marked social differences lay not between city and suburb, but among the suburbs.

The growth of the suburbs made it possible for people to segregate themselves on an ever increasing scale. Segregation is an elusive concept; for it can occur at many scales and can be measured in various ways. A group may be said to be segregated if its residential distribution differs from that of other groups. It is possible for a group to be highly segregated at one scale but to be quite integrated at another. An immigrant area, for example, may contain many blocks that are dominated by particular nationalities but that, overall, contain a great mixture of peoples. Is this an example of segregation or of mixing? There is no single answer, and to respond intelligently we need to be explicit about the scale of analysis that we consider important. Since the Second World War it has become common for sociologists and social geographers to measure segregation at the scale of the census tract, which has usually been the smallest scale at which most census data have been published. Since 1951, the first year that such data were reported for most Canadian cities, tract boundaries have been defined, first by the Dominion Bureau of Statistics and later by Statistics Canada, so as to create areas that are comparatively homogeneous in their social characteristics. On average they contain about 5,000 people (1,500–2,000 households) and, depending on the density of settlement, extend over a number of city blocks or an entire suburban subdivision.

Although many measures, or indices, of segregation have been devised, by far the most widely used is the index of segregation that was developed in the 1950s by Otis and Beverly Duncan. Easily calculated, this index also lends itself to a simple interpretation. It can vary between 0 and 100 (sometimes written 0–1.00). Index values may be interpreted as percentages. A value of 100 (or 1.0) indicates the presence of complete segregation: every member of the group in question would have to move in order for there to be no segregation. A value of 0 indicates that no one need move, because there is already no segregation. Innumerable studies have used the Duncans' index to determine the amount of segregation in Canadian and U.S. cities in the post-war period and have consistently found similar results. Measures of social class – usually occupation, income, and educational attainment – yield index values that range between about 10 and 35. Typically, the most segregated are those at each end of the class or income spectrum: the poor and the rich, or labourers and managers. The least segregated are those with intermediate levels of income and status, including white-collar and skilled manual workers. Often, ethnic or racial-

ized minorities show significantly higher levels of segregation. At the extreme, in U.S. cities African-Americans have
consistently experienced levels of segregation that exceed
80. In Canada, few groups have ever experienced levels of
segregation that high, although in some cities (notably
Montreal) the Jewish community has come close, and part
of the small Afro-Canadian community in Halifax was highly
segregated in the Africville district before the Second World
War. Commonly, groups that contain a large proportion of
first-generation immigrants show segregation levels in the
50s or 60s. Those groups that contain more people who are
in the second or subsequent generations show lower levels
of segregation, though ethnic segregation does persist for
many decades.

It is not possible to make precise comparisons between
the levels of segregation that have characterized post-war
metropolitan areas and those of pre-war cities and suburbs.
Small-area census data were not published before 1951,
and in Canada the nominal census is not available to
researchers beyond the 1901 census year. Fortunately, a few
scholars have used property assessment records to produce
estimates of class and ethnic segregation in specific cities,
and this fragmentary evidence does permit some generali-
zation. It is clear, for example, that segregation by ethnicity
has almost always been greater than segregation by social
class. In a study of Toronto in 1931, for example, Dan Hiebert found that the degree of class segregation varied from
a high of 48 for capitalists, to a low of 19 among skilled
workers. (He also reported an index value of 15 for the self-
employed; the latter group, not usually identified in post-
war analyses of segregation, included shopkeepers who
lived in all parts of the city.) These figures are quite high,
but levels of ethnic segregation were even higher, ranging
from a low of 28 for those of western and northern European background to a high of 65 for Jews. Hiebert found
similarly high levels of ethnic segregation in Winnipeg in
1901 and 1921. This does not necessarily mean that ethnic

segregation mattered more, but merely that it was more
marked.

Just as significant as the level of segregation was the
trend. Taken together, studies of Montreal, Winnipeg, and
Hamilton indicate that class segregation was increasing
steadily from the late nineteenth century until about the
Second World War. In a study of Montreal, Robert Lewis
found that in 1861 indices of occupational segregation
ranged from a high of 46 for the bourgeoisie, that is, merchants and manufacturers, to a low of about 17 for both
skilled and semi-skilled workers. These figures cannot be
compared directly with those of Hiebert for Toronto, since
Lewis was examining patterns at a smaller scale of analysis.
What is significant, however, is that segregation levels in
Montreal increased over the next forty years for almost all
occupational class groups. The segregation of skilled workers, for example, the second largest occupational category,
jumped from 17 to 26. The trend towards increasing segregation, which almost certainly affected the largest cities
first, continued in the early decades of the twentieth century. Hiebert found that in Winnipeg the segregation of
most occupation groups increased between 1901 and 1921.
The most telling information, however, has been provided
by Michael Doucet and John Weaver for Hamilton from
1856 to 1966. In the mid-nineteenth century levels of occupational segregation in Hamilton were relatively low. At the
ward scale, Doucet and Weaver report index values that
ranged from a high of 30 for 'professionals and proprietors' to a low of 21 for unskilled labour. Levels of segregation actually fell through the second half of the nineteenth
century, but then began to climb again around the turn of
the century. Except for skilled and semi-skilled workers,
they continued to rise into the post-war period. It is not
easy to discern broad trends from these local studies
because they differ in their period of coverage, their scales
of analysis, and also in the way that occupational categories
are defined. The most plausible interpretation, however, is

that a trend towards greater occupational class segregation appeared in the largest Canadian cities in the late nineteenth century. It began to affect medium-size centres such as Hamilton and Winnipeg in the early years of the twentieth century and continued into the early post-war years. This trend coincided with and was partly attributable to the rise of the suburbs.

Segregation mattered in a variety of ways. It was often preferred by recent immigrants, who found it useful and congenial to live in a community where people shared a language, cultural preferences, and religious institutions. Sociologists have shown that high levels of segregation have often been associated with a dense network of community institutions. In the first half of the twentieth century many immigrants settled in older city neighbourhoods. Jews, the largest 'foreign' immigrant population in most cities before the Second World War, were concentrated in districts like Toronto's 'Ward' and in the St Urbain corridor of Montreal. Quite a number, however, found their way very quickly into the suburbs. Winnipeg's North End, which extended out to the urban fringe, was a polyglot mix of eastern Europeans. In many centres, British immigrants often spent no more than a few months boarding downtown before buying a suburban lot, whether in York Township, Winnipeg's Elmwood district, or South Vancouver. In each place they created segregated communities. As members of most immigrant groups became established and moved into higher-class, more suburban districts, they often chose to remain segregated. This was true of the Jewish community in Toronto, as it migrated during the interwar years up the Bathurst corridor into Forest Hill and beyond; in Winnipeg after the Second World War, the Jewish community moved into West Kildonan and River Heights. In each case, new centres of segregated settlement made it easier to establish or relocate community institutions such as schools, churches, stores, and support systems. More typically, as second- and third-generation immigrants moved out of their ethnic ghettoes, they found their way into areas where ethnic identity mattered less. Until the 1970s the pressures to assimilate were strong, and the segregated ethnic community was viewed as a necessary but temporary phase, one that its members should struggle to transcend.

If ethnic segregation was supposed to be temporary, class segregation was a permanent feature of urban life. It created a situation where it was possible for wide differences in public services to develop. Even within a single municipality, where property owners might reasonably expect to be treated equally, such variations could affect living conditions, educational levels, and public health. For example, Patricia Thornton and Sherry Olson have shown that these differences existed in Montreal, where, partly as a result, rates of mortality were notably higher in the predominantly francophone districts, in which a supply of safe drinking water and milk was ensured later than in the anglophone districts that were so often home to the city's power brokers. Variations in public services were even greater among suburbs, and so were their effects.

Class segregation also mattered because it removed the sight (and smell) of poverty from the daily experience of the middle classes and the elite. Friedrich Engels had noted this aspect of the geography of Manchester, England, as early as the 1840s. As Engels described it, the new generation of mill owners in Manchester lived at the urban fringe and commuted by carriage into the centre along thoroughfares that were lined with shops and some of the better working-class housing. (It became common for builders to erect the cheapest housing along such thoroughfares only when they became very congested with streetcars and, later, with automobiles.) The poorest housing was tucked away on the back streets, out of sight, which Engels suggests allowed factory owners to ignore the working conditions of the poor and to continue to pay meagre wages with a clean conscience. Much the same argument was made half a century later by Herbert Ames in his study of Montreal. After noting that Montreal's 'city above the hill' contained 'the classes,' while the 'city below the hill' housed 'the masses,' Ames commented that 'most of the residents of the upper city know little – and at times seem to care less – regarding their fellow men in the city below.' In terms that echo Engels, Ames observed that 'to pass from the one [district] to the other only well-ordered thoroughfares are travelled. From this beaten track [the classes] seldom wander and of other regions they possess little or no knowledge.' The result, he suggests, was ignorance and complacency.

Friedrich Engels and Herbert Ames assumed that segregation helped to maintain the status quo. Most of the time they were probably right, but not always. The concentration of workers into particular districts made possible a dense network of associative life, a community. As Jane Synge has shown through her oral histories in Hamilton, neighbours and extended kin helped one another, while local storekeepers offered informal credit. The neighbourhood expressed a class experience outside the workplace and could solidify a collective identity. Just as segregation made it easier for immigrant communities to organize, it could perform the same function for workers, especially in periods of heightened conflict. The Winnipeg General Strike of 1919 was a prime example, although a complex one, since in that instance it was the combined segregation of immigrants and workers in the North End that seems to have fostered action. In political terms, then, the effects of segregation could cut either way.

Reformers drew the lesson that they needed to publicize the poor living conditions of the poor in order to mobilize middle-class opinion, perhaps before segregation encouraged workers to rebel. The most famous publicist in North America in the late nineteenth century was Jacob Riis, whose *How the Other Half Lives* (1890) included posed portraits of life in New York tenements. It was widely read in

Canada, where it was echoed in the Rev. H.S. Magee's comment about Toronto in 1911: 'one-half does not know how the other half lives.' He added, 'to thousands in Toronto a knowledge of conditions in the "Ward" ... would come as a surprise and a shock.' The political implications were spelt out most clearly by J.J. Kelso: 'often the better class of citizens do not know what is going on, so these wretched social conditions are allowed to grow until they become well-nigh intolerable.' Riis, Magee, Kelso, and Woodsworth assumed that if segregation led to ignorance and complacency, they should be able to galvanize middle-class opinion by presenting the facts. This assumption was a little naive. As Engels appreciated, segregation was not accidental, and ignorance suited many members of bourgeois society only too well. But they were surely right in supposing that segregation mattered. It kept people apart, and out of sight was out of mind. As the rise of the suburbs increased the extent and scale of segregation, it came to matter more.

Land Subdivision

If many people wished to be segregated, they were aided and abetted by the agents of land development. This process usually occurred in two phases: land subdivision and house building. Although these two steps may occur in a seamless sequence, this has not usually been the case in the past.

For land at the fringe to become available for urban land uses it must be surveyed and subdivided into building lots and the results made legal at the local registry office. Strictly speaking, the result is a registered plan. The terms 'subdivision' and 'survey' are used, although they also can refer to whole districts that grew up from a series of registered plans. The Westdale area of Hamilton, for example, is now thought of as a single district, even though it is the product of a land syndicate that registered no less than twelve plans between 1921 and 1940. In the nineteenth and early twentieth centuries land subdividers usually created rectangular lots within a street grid. This was the easiest approach and was consistent with the framework of rural lots and concessions from which urban subdivisions were usually carved. Most of those who subdivided land aimed to make quick money and showed little interest in what happened after lots were sold. They imposed few restraints on what could be done with the land, selling individual parcels to buyers who, in turn, looked to resell at a profit. Research by Michael Doucet and John Weaver in Hamilton indicates that in the late nineteenth century it was common for undeveloped parcels of suburban land to be traded at least five times before someone decided to build. Land was a commodity in which individuals speculated freely, especially during booms, when prices were rising rapidly. All levels of society became involved, including workers and widows, many of whom could afford only one or two parcels. People gambled with land the way that they now buy stocks or even lottery tickets.

Investors recognized that some parcels and subdivisions offered more security and better returns than others. In the language of the stock market, there were both blue-chip and penny stocks. Peter Moore has argued that by the 1880s middle-class buyers had come to expect new houses to have basic public services, including paved roads and sidewalks, piped water and sewers. By 1900 streetcar service was added to this list. Aware of these expectations, speculators paid a premium for serviced land, not simply because it was serviced but because it was likely to be developed earlier than nearby unserviced sites and would be attractive to families that could afford to pay a little over the odds. Those who first subdivided the land, therefore, did what they could to make sure that their subdivisions were given priority by the local municipality and streetcar companies. There was plenty of scope for back room wheeling and dealing.

Between the late nineteenth century and the 1950s many

land subdividers used other ways to enhance the marketability of building lots. The value of any parcel of urban
land depends on how adjacent parcels are used. A suburban house will be worth less if the neighbours build shacks
than if they build similar, or better, houses. It will be worth
still less if a neighbour sets up a piggery. Where land use is
unregulated, those who buy property can never be certain
about what their neighbours will do and hence what their
own property is worth. They will pay more for land in subdivisions where certain types of land use and inferior types
of house are prohibited. Here their investment is, at least
to some degree, guaranteed.

By the early 1900s land subdividers recognized that
they could charge a premium for lots that were covered by
legally enforceable deed restrictions. Such restrictions
might prohibit non-residential use or certain methods of
construction, for example, wood framing. Some of the
most common specified the minimum value that a dwelling
must have. In this way, developers could target specific
segments of the market. In most of Hamilton's Westdale
subdivisions, for example, the land syndicate specified a
minimum building value of $3,000, which produced a land-
scape of two- or two-and-a-half-storey brick homes in the
styles that were common in middle-class areas. In three
contiguous subdivisions they reduced this minimum to
$2,500, resulting in a more modest area of respectable bun-
galows. In three others they created an exclusive area
where lots were at least double the standard width and buyers had to build houses worth upwards of $7,000.

By defining the physical and economic character of a suburban district, building restrictions could be used to limit its
class composition. An example is the early twentieth-century
subdivisions in Toronto documented by Ross Paterson.
They ranged from Lawrence Park, which the developer
proclaimed to be 'restricted,' through the 'reasonably
restricted' area of Danforth-Woodbine, through Silverthorn
Park, where controls were 'very moderate,' to the Parsons

8   Subdivision advertisement for the Uplands, Victoria, 1912. In
advance of suburban municipalities, land developers introduced building and zoning regulations to reassure buyers in the better subdivisions
that their investments would be secure. (*Victoria Daily Colonist*, 9 May
1912. Courtesy of L.D. McCann)

Estate in York Township, where there were 'no restrictions' whatsoever. The social consequences were predictable. By 1931 in these four areas, respectively, blue-collar workers made up 1 per cent, 50 per cent, 75 per cent, and 90 per cent of all male household heads. Through private controls, developers modulated the physical and class character of their subdivisions and contributed to the growth of social segregation.

Private development controls had their greatest impact in western cities. In the early 1900s the Hudson's Bay Company owned 50,000 acres around the sites of its original forts in Winnipeg, Edmonton, and the Princes Albert, George, and Rupert. The CPR also owned vast tracts in suburban Winnipeg, Calgary, and Vancouver. The success of John Olmsted's plans for The Uplands in Victoria encouraged the land agents for these companies to hire Olmsted and/or his associates to design similar subdivisions elsewhere. In most western centres, then, favoured areas emerged where a bucolic aesthetic was backed by regulations that defined and maintained a certain social cachet.

The one aspect of a subdivision that building controls could not influence, except indirectly, was its ethnic composition. Prejudice against ethnic and racialized minorities was the norm in the early twentieth century. Most immigrants came from the British Isles, and others were regarded as 'foreigners.' The most numerous were Italians, Jews, and, on the west coast, the Chinese. Anglo- and Franco-Canadians viewed all of these groups with suspicion and imputed to them questionable morals and practices. Each of these immigrant groups first settled in segregated immigrant ghettoes, usually close to the centre of the city. In each case, the choice was only partially voluntary. As Kay Anderson has shown for Vancouver's Chinese community, segregation was a defensive measure, a means of preserving self-esteem and identity as well as of limiting conflict.

Although many 'foreign' immigrants 'knew their place,' the developers of middle-class suburbs included covenants that explicitly excluded them. In Westdale, for example, John Weaver reports that covenants listed 'Negroes, Asiatics, Bulgarians, Austrians, Russians, Serbs, Rumanians, Turks, Armenians, whether British subjects or not' as well as 'foreign-born Italians, Greeks, or Jews' as groups that were unwelcome. Such elaborate lists were probably rare: what plausible threat did Armenians, whether British subjects or not, pose to the ethnic purity of suburban Canada in the interwar years? But it was easy to include such specifications, and in abbreviated form they were common. The targets varied from place to place, depending upon the composition of the local migrant and immigrant population. In the United States, those of African ancestry were usually singled out. According to James Walker, the same was true in Canada, particularly on the east coast, but out west 'Orientals' were commonly mentioned, while in many cities their place was taken by Jews. Indeed, Walter van Nus suggests that in Montreal 'restricted' simply meant 'no Jews.'

Racial covenants were not always enforced. Jim Pask reports an ironic case in East Kildonan, outside Winnipeg. There, H.M. Milland bought land from George Mohr, a German immigrant. He subdivided the tract and sold lots, but only to people born in Canada, Britain, or the United States. He nevertheless used Mohr's name, suitably anglicized, to designate the area Morse Place. This irony was compounded after the project ran into financial difficulties during the First World War. Properties were abandoned by their owners and poor Ukrainians moved in. Soon the area, which lay on the east side of the railway tracks, became ostracized by British-Canadians on the west side. Covenants were effective only where there was ample and steady demand by the ethnic majority. Conversely, they were not always required. A fine example was the Kingsway area in central Etobicoke. The developer styled it 'Angliae par Anglia procul' – a little bit of England away from England – and did not trouble to include racial covenants. No one who failed to fit the image would have bothered, or perhaps dared, to apply. But although covenants were not always needed, they were widely deployed and continued to have an influence even after the Supreme Court of Canada declared them illegal in 1950. It has been said, for example, that they discouraged Jews from settling in the eastern sections of Toronto, so that, by default, when the Jewish community began to expand in the interwar years, it moved northward into Forest Hill and points beyond. The sectoral pattern established in the early decades of this century is still apparent today. Together with private building restrictions, ethnic covenants shaped the patterns of settlement in many Canadian urban areas.

Although building restrictions increased the value of land in most subdivisions, they were not universally adopted in the early twentieth century. The demand for the better subdivisions was finite. Lower-income families were more likely to be attracted by the absence of regulation, as many land subdividers recognized. In Toronto, the Dovercourt Land, Building and Savings Company, which created Lawrence Park, was also responsible for the Parsons Estate, and in the latter area it made the absence of regulation a selling point. Westdale embodied the regulated middle-class ideal in Hamilton's west end, while to the east unregulated surveys such as Union Park catered to the families of those who worked in the nearby steel mills. We do not know how many subdivisions, like Union Park, were completely unrestricted. The only systematic study that has been undertaken of any North American city indicates that in Wilmington, Delaware, in the first decade of this century, about half of all subdivisions had some type of restriction, although in some cases they were quite minimal. It is likely that the proportion of unrestricted subdivisions was higher in Canadian cities, especially in the west, where in the years leading up to the First World War, many subdividers were intent on cashing in on the speculative boom. They were less interested in shaping neighbourhoods than in creating marketable plots for quick sale to the next gullible investor in Toronto or Aberdeen.

The absence of any private or public controls on land subdivision became a serious concern after the economy rebounded from the sharp recession of 1907–8. Observers were struck by several developments. First and foremost was an extraordinary speculative spiral in land prices. The biggest increases occurred west of the Ontario-Manitoba border. In Transcona, Winnipeg, land prices jumped from $6.50 per front foot before work on the repair shops began in 1910 to $125 per front foot in 1912. Charles Forward reports that between 1906 and 1912 the value of a sixty-foot lot in Fairfield, Victoria, rose tenfold, from $500 to $5,000. Absurd price inflation affected even the smaller urban areas. A.G. Dalzell calculated that in Fort William (now Thunder Bay) in 1907 'foreigners' were paying more on a front foot basis for 'treeless swamp' in the coal docks section than families had to spend to acquire property in Hampstead Garden Suburb, a well-planned and prestigious suburb of London, England. Perhaps the best indication of the overall pattern is the trend in assessed values for suburban South Vancouver. In 1920, a few years after the boom had gone bust, A.H. Lewis reported that the assessed value of all property in South Vancouver had grown from just over $1 million in 1900 to more than $33 million in 1912, despite the loss incurred through the annexation of Point Grey into the City of Vancouver. As prices rose, workers were continually forced to seek cheaper land further out, even though more convenient sites were available. Even then, as the medical officer of health in Regina commented, 'by the time many of these people ... have bought their lots, they could not afford to build anything better than a shack for a home.' Speculators obliged by creating more lots still further out, and so the vicious cycle continued ... for a time.

Like all speculative booms, the spiral of suburban land prices eventually crashed. The assessed value of property in

South Vancouver was halved between 1912 and 1919. Since assessors would have been cautious about reassessing properties downward, the actual decline in property values was probably greater. Tens of thousands of people were left holding land that was worth less than they had paid and for which there was no market. Many had hoped to hold their land for only a few weeks or months, at most a year or two. Even those who could afford to keep paying their property taxes soon became disinclined to do so. Between 1918 and 1921 the owners of 44,348 parcels of land in Edmonton stopped paying taxes and allowed their property to fall into the unwilling hands of the municipality. The market recovered in the 1920s, but not by enough. By then Edmonton owned four-fifths of all the vacant sites in the city, mostly at or beyond the urban fringe. Even in eastern cities the consequences were serious. The municipality of Nepean had acquired hundreds of lots through tax arrears by the early 1920s, and the same pattern was reproduced in most suburban districts.

While it lasted, the land boom produced irrational and expensive patterns of suburban settlement. It encouraged developers to create more lots than were needed, and families leapfrogged over vacant land to acquire cheaper lots at the fringe. Whole areas of Calgary and Edmonton that were subdivided before 1913 lay vacant until after 1945. John Saywell reports that in Toronto one subdivision that was advertised before the First World War still lay undeveloped in 1960. No contemporary documented this pattern of settlement more exhaustively, or railed against it more eloquently, than the consulting engineer and planner A.G. Dalzell. As Dalzell pointed out, the main problem was that widely scattered development was difficult and expensive to service. He gathered, and possibly embellished, a number of examples to illustrate his point. In Vancouver's Ward 8, for example, he reckoned that the cost of providing basic municipal services exceeded the value of land and, more significantly, also was greater than the cost of servicing

Shaughnessy Heights, an area with better services and larger lots. The problems were poor street layout and, even more, the cost of installing services after development had already begun. In Winnipeg, he calculated that in the mid-1920s among the nine suburban municipalities only one in every thirteen lots was developed, and of these only half were connected to sewers. Because of scattered development, this meant that many vacant lots had sewerage while many houses lacked connections. Neither situation made sense.

The absence of sewer connections was a health hazard, especially in areas that drew drinking water from wells. The hazard grew rapidly as areas were settled. In parts of York Township, northeast and northwest of Toronto, there was large-scale development between about 1910 and the early 1920s before water lines and sewers finally were installed. Here, as in many other Canadian suburbs, families used privies and shared wells. It is not clear whether this arrangement often caused health problems, but in some cases it certainly did. The best known case occurred in Ottawa, where typhoid epidemics in 1911 and 1912 were traced to surface pollution from outdoor privies in Hintonburg. Subsurface water from the privies drained into Cave Creek and thence into the Ottawa River, just above the water intake for the city. What is surprising is that such incidents were not more common.

The provision of services to vacant land in scattered settlements was a financial disaster. Strathcona, an extensive district south of Edmonton that was annexed in 1913, was a classic case. Partly as a means of promoting development, and partly in response to the subsequent scattering of settlement, Strathcona spent freely to build bridges, fire halls, and water and sewer systems. These expenditures pushed its debt from $24,000 in 1900 to $200,000 in 1906 and $1,294,000 by 1912. The pattern was general and, in order to repay or even service such debt, suburban municipalities had to raise taxes several times over. Many homeowners found that they could not afford to pay, and they joined the speculative owners of vacant lots by falling into arrears. By the mid-1920s a large minority of home owners in York Township and East York were behind in their tax payments. A vicious cycle had already been established. Arrears forced municipalities to raise taxes further, which increased the number of owners who became delinquent. Municipalities were not eager to acquire vacant land abandoned by speculators, and they did everything they could not to evict families, even when they were owed several years of back taxes. From every point of view the situation was a mess.

As the social, economic, and fiscal consequences of unregulated development became apparent during the 1910s, more than ever those who laid out new subdivisions found it necessary to reassure buyers. Increasing numbers of developers imposed restrictions that offered buyers the guarantee of respectable neighbours. During the 1900s building restrictions were used in the prestigious suburban developments. By the 1920s they were being routinely deployed in middle-class areas such as Westdale. A taste for the 'Garden Suburb' style also filtered down, commonly in the form of curvilinear street designs that helped to provide the suburb with a focus, either a shopping district, community centre, or school. Hamilton's Westdale was a good example. To some degree, therefore, developers responded to the problems of unregulated development by offering their private version of planning.

House Building

Although land subdividers began to exert control over how the suburbs were developed, until the Second World War they did not set an example by building houses. In the nineteenth century, the builder was the last of many owners of a piece of land and he – almost all builders were men – made his own decisions about what to build. In the restricted subdivisions and more cautious land market of the 1920s vacant land changed hands less often, while builders had to pay attention to whatever covenants the subdivider had defined. Still, entrepreneurs usually specialized in land subdivision or building, but not both.

In the early decades of the twentieth century, suburban houses were assembled by one of three types of builder. The most common type operated speculatively, in the sense that he started to build before he had a buyer. To finance this operation he usually had to borrow money from a local lending institution. Construction loans might be phased, so that money was advanced in stages as the building project proceeded. Building 'on spec' was risky. Buying a house was a major investment and required confidence in future prosperity; for houses typically cost about three times the family's annual income. Even slight downturns in the economy had a disproportionate effect on the housing market. A builder might start a house in the spring, and by the time he completed it in late summer the beginnings of an economic downturn might have encouraged potential buyers to postpone their plans. To stay flexible during the inevitable downturns, speculative builders kept their workforce to a minimum by subcontracting to specialized trades. For Westdale, John Weaver reports in some detail the activities of Thomas Casey, a medium-size builder who erected about eighty houses between 1920 and 1955. In the 1920s he dug basements and framed houses, but left most of the finishing work to 'the seven trades': masons, lathers, plasterers, electricians, plumbers, roofers, and tinsmiths.

To further minimize risk, builders like Casey used the standard designs that sold well and concentrated on the middle segments of the housing market, where there were the largest number of families that could afford to buy. They were most active in larger cities, where demand was most predictable. It was only in these centres that speculative builders operated on a substantial scale. Even so, the majority built no more than five houses a year. It was a very

9   Speculatively built interwar housing in Westdale, Hamilton. Later
additions do not disguise the uniformity of this row of middle-class
houses in the 'four-square' style that was common just before and after
the First World War. Such uniformity is a good clue that they were
erected by a speculative builder using a standard building plan.
Architects played little or no role in designing most suburban housing.
(Richard Harris)

rare builder who would take on as many as fifty dwellings in
a season. Most blocks and all subdivisions of any size were
developed by several, and sometimes dozens, of builders.
In Westdale, at least thirty builders were active. On average,
over a period of twenty years each built about fifty houses.

Although the technology of construction evolved slowly,
during the 1920s some of the larger speculative builders
began to refine their marketing. In the very early years of
this century, some companies began to sell kit homes by
mail order. Kits contained everything needed to build a
house, including lumber, nails, wiring, pipes, and instruc-
tions. The earliest and best known of these manufacturers,

Aladdin Company and Sears, Roebuck and Company, were based in the United States, but also sold to Canadians. Canadian companies soon joined in the competition. By 1910 they included the T. Eaton Company and, on the west coast, B.C. Mills. A disproportionate number of kits were sold on the prairies, where, especially in the smaller communities, the local building industry was too small to meet the demand. Kit manufacturers made inroads everywhere. Part of their appeal was their capacity to sell 'homes,' not merely houses: catalogues showed images, sometimes in colour, of finished and furnished dwellings. For its day this was slick advertising, and, to compete, in the 1920s some builders went one better by erecting 'model homes' on site. These models became effective marketing tools, but only for a few. Most builders operated on too small a scale and with too limited capital to tie up thousands of dollars in a three-dimensional catalogue.

One way of minimizing the amount of capital that builders required was to operate on demand, rather than 'on spec.' On the heels of the speculative builder, then, was the second type, the custom builder or general contractor, who built for particular clients. He often received an up-front retainer followed by a series of progress payments as each stage of construction was completed: the foundation, frame, roof, and interior finishing. As Ross Paterson has described, in Kingsway Park, except for the framing, the custom builder would usually delegate each of these tasks to subcontractors. (Most builders were carpenters by trade.) From the builder's point of view, this method of operation almost eliminated the need for capital and also the element of risk. The client family, in return, received a house that fit its particular needs and preferences. This approach offered benefits all round, but it did cost more. From the client's point of view, the whole point of hiring a general contractor was to build a house with distinctive design, features, or materials. Consultations took time, especially if clients had to be educated about the relative

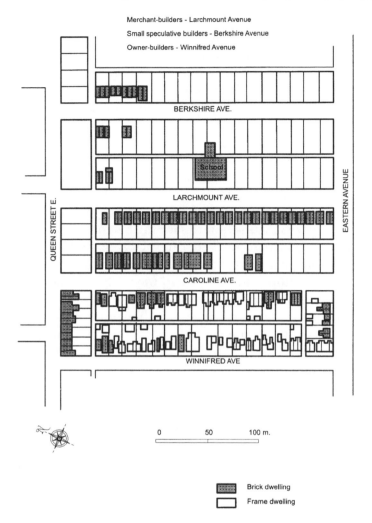

10   Different builders produced varied streetscapes, east Toronto, 1920s. Identical pairs of houses on Larchmount Avenue were produced by a medium-size speculative builder. Individual pairs on Berkshire and Caroline Avenues were erected speculatively or on contract by small professional builders. The irregular streetscape along Winnifred Avenue reflects the activity of amateurs. The Goad insurance atlases are a source of detailed and useful information about suburban development. (Redrawn from Charles E. Goad, *Atlas of the City of Toronto and Suburbs* [Toronto: Goad, 1910; rev. to 1924])

costs of different materials or the possible inconveniences of an idiosyncratic design. To facilitate the process the client might hire an architect – an additional cost. For these reasons, custom builders operated largely in the upper segments of the housing market, although in smaller communities they also built more modest houses to standard designs.

Custom and speculative builders, who together constituted the construction industry, built for the minority of the population that could afford to buy a new house. Until the Second World War, buyers were able to borrow no more than about half of the cost of a new house, and only a minority were in a position to save the balance. Then again, even the better-paid workers often lacked the job security that lenders preferred. The majority of families could hope to acquire a house in one of two ways. They could buy an older building, perhaps in a neighbourhood that had declined in value. Alternatively, if they wanted to move to the suburbs, they could build their own dwelling. Those who erected houses for their own use were the third, common type of builder.

Owner-builders were responsible for a large minority of the suburban dwellings that were built in Canada in the first three decades of the twentieth century. From a detailed study of Toronto I concluded that about two-fifths of all of the new, single-family houses in the boom period 1900–13 were owner built. The proportion was markedly higher in suburban areas and in western Canada. By building their own houses, families made home ownership more affordable in two ways. Using personal labour, they pared building costs to a minimum of land and materials, although some hired tradesmen to perform the more skilled tasks, such as wiring. Also, by building in stages, amateurs reduced the need for savings or credit. Many started with nothing more than a one-room shack, which was extended, improved, and perhaps replaced, as finances allowed. A common pattern was for a family to build a shack at the back of the lot and then make it a shed when later they built a substantial house at the front. For example, Joseph Thorne: born in London, England, Thorne left his family and journeyed to Canada in 1905. After working off a farm indenture, he moved to Toronto, where he soon bought a suburban lot. He dug a basement, covered it with tin, and then sent home for his wife and five children. By the time they arrived in 1907, he had built a two-room shack with a dirt floor. In time he learned how to lay bricks, built a stone house for his family, and was employed as a bricklayer at Casa Loma, Henry Pellatt's famous Toronto mansion. Like Joseph Thorne, many owner-builders ended up in the building trades, but most were self-taught. If speculative builders concentrated their efforts in the middle of the market, and general contractors worked for clients at the upper end, amateur builders were responsible for the great mass of the cheapest houses, including those that middle-class contemporaries dismissed as 'shacks.'

Four Types of Suburb

In principle, the diverse methods of land subdivision and house building could have created an almost infinite variety of suburbs. In practice, certain combinations were more likely than others. Three were especially common and helped to create four distinct types of physical and social environment.

The most prominent, but not the most common, type of suburb was the affluent enclave. Here, the influence of the Olmsteds and of Garden City styles was felt very early, including Mount Royal, Montreal, the only suburb in Canada to be designed by Olmsted senior, and John Olmsted's South Mount Royal in Calgary. Subdividers laid out large lots on curving streets and made ample provision for parks and other green spaces. They arranged for municipal services to be installed at the same time as the first houses were being built. By imposing tight building restrictions, they were able to define quite precisely the physical appearance of the area. Sometimes, as in Shaughnessy Heights' and Westmount, this influence was backed up by architectural controls. Such restrictions established the area's tone and, together with racial covenants, defined its social composition. Almost invariably, houses were built by general contractors, often working with architects. Affluent families could afford to pay the premium and competed in erecting distinguished, and distinctive, dwellings. In such areas, the suburban landscape was gracious and varied.

At the other extreme was the unplanned suburb. Lots usually had narrow frontages of twenty to thirty feet, defined within an unimaginative grid. Subdividers concerned themselves very little with municipal services. They rarely bothered to define building regulations and often used the absence of regulation as a selling point. Especially in the early years, the absence of regulation defined the physical and social character of these subdivisions almost as effectively as tight controls shaped the affluent enclave. Speculative builders generally avoided such areas, because the absence of controls undercut demand for the sorts of housing that could profitably be built. Instead, in York Township and South Vancouver, in Hintonburg (Nepean) and Hillhurst (Calgary), in Cobalt (Ontario) and Elmwood (Manitoba), as well as in Africville, Nova Scotia, unplanned suburbs were almost entirely developed by amateurs. The landscape was varied, though within definite limits. Most amateurs did not set out to build distinctive houses, but peculiarities of taste and circumstance often yielded that effect. As Alice Randle commented of the houses in York Township late in 1913, 'no two are alike,' since the owners had consulted 'their individual needs and tastes alone ... and so each cottage seemed to have a personality all its own.' Because owners were building in stages, sometimes at first on the back of the lot, a block might contain everything from shacks to respectable two-storey dwellings, the latter boasting varied setbacks from the street. Middle-class observers deplored such homespun anarchy as ugly or even ludicrous. In 1920 a Montreal contributor to *Social Welfare*, the journal for the nascent Canadian social work profession, condemned it as 'grotesque improvisation.' A minority, including Randle, overlooked such deficiencies, interpreting unplanned suburbs as steps towards a brighter future.

Between these extremes were two types of suburb in which speculative builders were usually dominant. The first was the industrial suburb, whether planned or unplanned. The development of an industrial suburb offered builders the prospect of a boom in demand for modest, but standard houses. From the builder's point of view, the ideal was a place like Maisonneuve, where local industries and land developers commissioned the construction of a few houses, which were then rented. This sort of custom building for corporate clients was the builder's ideal. A prominent example was the Hydrostone district in Halifax, which had been levelled by the disastrous naval explosion in 1917. With federal assistance the district was rebuilt, in effect as a low-rise rental project, for those who had lost their homes. Government contracts specified the use of new concrete block materials, known as Hydrostone and also the use of novel designs. The result was an unusually uniform area. Less ideal from the builder's point of view, but still attractive, were districts such as the West Toronto Junction or the east end of Hamilton. Land subdividers in these areas knew that builders, as much as home buyers, would want some reassurance. As a result, in places like Silverthorn Park, which was adjacent to the Junction, they specified some modest restrictions. Of course, housing for the better-paid industrial workers was not very profitable on a per unit basis, but quantity production compensated for small margins. The concentration of new jobs in industrial suburbs offered builders a predictable, captive market. These were conditions under which some builders ventured to operate on a large scale, creating unimaginative and utilitarian streetscapes.

The other type of subdivision in which speculative builders were dominant was targeted at the middle class by land
developers. Before the First World War, such areas might
be gridded; after 1918 they were more likely to contain curvilinear streets as well as small parks. The demonstration
effect of the more prestigious suburbs was very apparent.
However, lots in middle-class subdivisions were only a little
more generous than in the unregulated districts or industrial suburbs, largely because most families still commuted
on foot or by transit. These were areas from which commuters might have to travel some distance to work, and
they had to compete with other areas for the home buyer's
business. Builders could not rely on large-scale demand.
They were reassured by subdividers, who imposed moderate restrictions, and they kept their risks low by building
only a few dwellings per year. The result was a predictable
landscape Although less utilitarian and sometimes less uniform than the industrial suburb, it was dominated by versions of the favoured styles of the day. In Ontario these
included Queen Anne influences before the First World
War, soon followed by the stolid, two-and-a-half-storey four-
square, built of solid brick or brick veneer. The bungalow
influence was felt in the longer, more shallowly pitched
roofs of the 1920s. In western Canada, as Deryck Holdsworth has shown, the California bungalow had become
popular earlier and was expressed in a wider variety of
styles, sometimes with exuberantly overhanging eaves.
There was regional variety, but within each middle-class
subdivision – in Westdale, as in the more moderately
priced districts of Point Grey, such as Kerrisdale – the
dominant impression was one of variations on a theme.

Elite, unplanned, industrial, and middle class all were
recognizable types of the early twentieth-century suburb.
Whether because of deed restrictions, financial constraints,
or the standardizing logic of speculative house building,
each tended to display a significant degree of homogeneity, if not always in their physical appearance, then in their

class composition. Subdivided and built in a variety of styles, they were occupied by different classes of people and were strikingly different in appearance. Individually homogeneous, they were collectively diverse.

Canadian Peculiarities

None of the four main types of suburb was distinctively Canadian, but the balance among them was. By comparison with U.S. cities, those in Canada depended more on trade and less on manufacturing. As a result, industrial suburbs were not as common. Because of slightly lower incomes and rates of car ownership so, too, were elite and middle-class suburbs. On the other hand, unplanned suburbs were so widespread that the first government-sponsored urban renewal scheme was imposed, during the 1950s, in Kingston's Rideau Heights, a suburban shacktown. Owner-building, especially by immigrant workers, clearly was an unusually prominent feature of the Canadian suburban scene.

Unregulated settlement was both a consequence and also a cause of a peculiarly Canadian pattern of house financing. Houses were (and are) so expensive that most families must borrow in order to buy. When the McCalls bought their first house in Winnipeg in 1912, for example, they put $700 down and borrowed the remaining $3,700. By Canadian standards, however, this case was unusual. In the first three decades of the twentieth century most families could not borrow much more than half of the value of their house, although quite a few did take out second mortgages on which they had to pay a higher rate of interest. (In the event of a default, the holder of a first mortgage had top priority; thus, whoever provided a second mortgage demanded a premium for the higher risk.) It was also common for borrowers to repay loans quickly, which the system encouraged. The usual mortgage ran for only five years, and during this term the borrower paid only the interest on the loan. At the end of the term the full amount of the principal was still owed, and, if the borrower had not saved the full amount, a new mortgage had to be negotiated, perhaps with a new lender. This cumbersome system, coupled with a widespread cultural aversion to debt, encouraged families to borrow no more than necessary and to repay their loans as soon as possible.

Much the same system of mortgage lending prevailed across North America, but Canadian buyers differed from their U.S. counterparts in relying more heavily on other individuals for credit, rather than using lending institutions. In the United States in the early decades of this century, most buyers borrowed from local banks or savings and loan companies, of the sort that Frank Capra showed so sympathetically in the 1946 movie *It's a Wonderful Life*. In Canada, however, after a lending crisis in the 1870s, the federal government prohibited banks from lending on the security of real estate. At first, trust as well as building and loans companies picked up the slack. Like the American savings and loans firms, the latter specialized in the provision of mortgages. Unlike them, however, they drew capital from overseas, chiefly from England and Scotland, rather than from local depositors. When, for a variety of reasons, the main sources of British capital dried up after the First World War, the building and loans companies went into a rapid decline. The shortage of institutional funds in Canada forced many buyers to look elsewhere. Some were helped by members of their extended families, while those who bought older buildings were sometimes able to obtain 'take-back' mortgages from the vendors. The majority, however, approached local lawyers or, in Quebec, *notaires publiques*, who put them in touch with individuals who happened to have some money to spare. Probably this was the route by which Arthur Evans found Alderman Twiss. However, private lenders were not necessarily prominent or rich. Many were widows, and in general the majority were men and women who had managed to accumulate a modest sum and wished to place it in a secure, local investment.

Throughout the first half of the century, more than 50 per cent of all residential mortgages in Canada were provided by private individuals, a much higher proportion than in the United States or than is common today.

The shortage of institutional mortgage finance in Canada encouraged owner-building in unplanned suburbs. If families could not borrow and they wanted to own a new house, the only option was to build one themselves. Professional builders, too, were affected, and perhaps more seriously. In the United States, savings and loans companies and banks routinely provided builders with construction loans. In Canada, it appears that the chartered banks were not involved in this sort of business. Since private individuals would have much preferred to lend on the security of a finished house, it is likely that builders in Canadian cities were unusually hampered by a shortage of credit. Almost by default, then, a great deal of building was left to amateurs. There was also a reciprocal effect. As long as so much suburban development was able to proceed with little need of credit, lending institutions and the federal government were able to turn their attention elsewhere. In the early decades of the twentieth century, self-financing and unregulated development helped to define one of the most distinctive elements of the Canadian suburban scene.

The mix of suburban development evolved steadily between 1900 and 1929, as unplanned expansion was slowly displaced during the 1920s by the growth of middle-class suburbs. It was the Great Depression, however, that precipitated a more dramatic shift. The single most important development in this period was stimulated by a change in the system of mortgage finance. However, this shift was eventually tied to significant changes in the methods of land subdivision and house building. In all of these respects, initiatives taken by the federal government were eventually to prove decisive.

5

The Growing Influence of the State

In the early twentieth century, suburbs were diverse because governments allowed them to be. The federal government had no direct effect on the way urban areas developed. In the 1910s provincial governments began to pass legislation that purported to control how subdivisions were laid out, but they were largely ineffectual. Suburban diversity was fostered by the fragmentation and variability of local government, not only between city and suburb but also among the suburbs. It was only when the federal government entered the housing field in 1935, when local governments began to adopt national building standards in the 1940s, and when provincial governments brought in more rigorous planning legislation after 1945, that Canadian suburbs started to earn their modern reputation for being homogeneous and bland. Diversity was slowly ironed out by the growing influence of the state.

The Promotion of Diversity

Until the 1930s federal and provincial governments played a minor role in the shaping of Canadian cities and suburbs. In European countries, national legislation had given local governments important powers by 1914. In Britain, for example, the Housing and Town Planning Act of 1909 was a landmark in theory and in practice. Moreover, when local governments began to plan and build large council (public) housing estates after the First World War, they directly shaped suburban development.

European initiatives were echoed in Canada, but faintly. In 1909 the prime minister, Wilfrid Laurier, established the Commission of Conservation and appointed Clifford Sifton as chair. Its purpose was to advise the government on the use of physical resources, but its mandate also included human resources. Dr Charles Hodgetts was appointed advisor on public health. Early discussions acknowledged the need for urban planning, and in 1914 Sifton appointed a Scot, Thomas Adams, as town planning advisor to the commission. Adams was one of the leading planners of the day. In Britain he had been secretary of the company that had tried to build the first Garden City, at Letchworth; he had helped to secure passage of the 1909 Planning Act; and he was founder and first president of the British Town Planning Institute in 1914. His arrival in Canada had a galvanizing effect. His activities with the commission and his writing for the commission's journal, *Town Planning and Conservation of Life*, raised the profile of the planning profession and led to the formation of the Town Planning Institute of Canada in 1919.

It was in 1919 that Adams was given the opportunity to influence more directly the way in which Canadian suburbs were being developed. In many countries, the disruptions of wartime created unrest. Some European governments built public housing for returning soldiers – 'homes for heroes' as they were known in Britain. Faced with civil unrest in Winnipeg and elsewhere, Robert Borden's government took similar although more cautious steps. A short-lived national program provided funds that the provinces channelled to local housing commissions, which either built homes for sale or loaned money to individual families, who made arrangements with general contractors. (In a few cases, as in York Township, they also assisted owner-builders.) The public rhetoric indicated that the program was intended to help all veterans, but only the families of better-paid workers could afford to buy houses in a period of rapid inflation. Influenced by Adams, the federal government encouraged housing commissions to adopt advanced ideas about subdivision planning. Adams himself designed a demonstration suburb at Lindenlea in Ottawa. Drawing on Garden City ideas, it incorporated curvilinear streets, culs-de-sac, and tree-lined boulevards, while 10 per cent of the subdivision was set aside for several small parks, a children's playground, a wading pool, a bowling green, and tennis courts. The impact of this model, however, was limited. In most cities, including Toronto and Hamilton, commissions acquired lots in areas that already had been subdivided on a grid plan. They built houses inspired by British fashions in architecture, but the scale was smaller than that of British housing estates, and the effect on suburban development was minor.

By the early 1920s federal interest in planning was waning. Arthur Meighen's government abolished the Commission of Conservation in 1921, and in 1923 Adams moved to New York, where he became director of the Regional Plan. The national interest in planning during the 1910s had left a small legacy at the provincial level. In 1912–13 four provinces – New Brunswick, Nova Scotia, Ontario, and Alberta – passed planning acts that were based on British precedent, and within a decade four others had followed suit. The concern was to establish order to the manner in which suburban development occurred, both in controlling the overall pattern of development and in the narrower context of street patterns within each subdivision. On paper, this legislation looked impressive. In practice, as David Hulchanski, the historian of Ontario's early legislation, has commented, the provisions were ineffective. The unregulated subdivision boom that led up to 1912 shaped suburban development during the 1920s, and little was built during the 1930s and early 1940s. For a quarter-century, provincial planning legislation was largely a dead letter.

It was only at the municipal level that governments played a significant and growing role in the way that suburbs developed. By 1914 the governments of the larger Canadian cities had instituted controls over development within city limits. Building regulations were devised in response to the threat of fire, but as reformers raised concerns about public health, by-laws also regulated ventilation, waste disposal, and noise. Cities outlawed privies and mandated the use of piped water and sewers. By the 1910s they were actually enforcing such legislation.

The situation in the suburbs was more diverse. Each of the four types of suburb that were discussed in the previous chapter had its own approach to government development. Exclusive suburbs depended on stringent zoning and building controls, the former to specify the types of land use that were permitted and the latter to regulate how structures should be built. Here, government was a tool for exclusion. Unplanned suburbs grew because their governments were unable or unwilling to take control of development. At first, they were dominated by farmers who preferred not to incur the expense of urban infrastructure; later they were controlled by low-income owner-builders who were also eager to keep taxes low. The governments of industrial suburbs were sometimes in the enviable position of having a good tax base, but they were deterred from imposing strict building regulations by their knowledge that only workers would be willing to put up with the noise and smells of nearby factories. Middle-income residential suburbs steered a careful middle path. In principle, each suburb had its own type of government and served a market niche; in practice, of course, things were rarely so clear-cut.

The mixed ecology of local governance that persisted through the 1920s was unstable. In particular, the unplanned suburb proved to be non-viable. Households could not settle at high densities without public services; when services were installed, too many households discov-

ered that they could not afford the necessary taxes; and
when households stopped paying taxes, municipal finances
began a downward spiral. Many of these problems could
have been avoided: subdivision regulations might have
kept settlement compact, while minimal services might
have been installed much more cheaply in advance of
development. Instead, unplanned suburbs found themselves in increasing difficulty during the 1920s. Around
Toronto the two largest unplanned suburbs, York and East
York, lobbied for annexation, but they were rebuffed by the
City. When the Great Depression struck, along with most of
the other Toronto suburbs and many others across the
country they went bankrupt. The crisis in municipal
finances reflected the larger economic disaster, but it was
just as surely a result of the pattern of suburban development and government that had evolved in previous
decades. Something had to change.

The Crisis of the Great Depression

It is difficult for us, who enjoy the security of insurance programs that cover ill health, unemployment, and perhaps
also our mortgage payments and who, should everything
else fail, can apply for social welfare, to appreciate just how
catastrophic the Great Depression was. Careers and lives
were put on hold when mere survival occupied every wak-
ing moment. It would be easy to assume that the greatest
hardship was experienced in the inner-city tenement, but
the truth was often otherwise. City tenants had the solace of
street-corner society and perhaps the church mission. They
were mobile and could miss rent payments and skip out in
the middle of the night. Suburban owners were more isolated, saddled with property they could not sell and debts
they could not repay. Theirs was at once a more private
misery and also a more consequential dilemma. During the
brief economic downturn of 1907–8 a cartoon in a Toronto
newspaper showed a wintry suburban scene of a tarpaper

shack with a large wolf at the door. Without jobs or welfare cheques, families depended on charity, which was hard to come by in newer settlements. The community resources available to suburban residents during the prolonged Depression of the 1930s were hardly an improvement. In the end, like Arthur Evans, many lost their homes. There was little that local governments could do about this situation. Suburban municipalities were under acute financial pressure and in no position to offer much welfare. Many refrained from taking possession of properties whose owners were in tax arrears. Such restraint was partly a matter of social conscience, but also one of calculation: there were few prospective buyers, and by acquiring properties the municipalities became responsible for upkeep. Apart from their reluctance to take away property from the unfortunate, therefore, they were in no position to offer much in the way of positive assistance.

As the actions of other nations showed, it was the federal government that was in the best position to mitigate and help to resolve the economic crisis. In the United States, some believed that the Depression had been prolonged by the manner in which urban development had occurred and also by the way it had been financed. Poorly planned subdivisions were risky investments that readily lost value; short-term balloon mortgages had to be renegotiated and invited termination; in the United States these circumstances encouraged foreclosure, the failure of many savings and loan companies, and a deepening financial crisis. To many, it seemed that a reformed real estate industry might lead the economy out of the Depression. House construction was labour intensive and enjoyed extensive backward and forward linkages: it created a demand for building materials and finance as well as for home furnishings and appliances. If suburban development had exacerbated the Depression, it also offered an activist government a lever with which to turn the economy around. Beginning in 1933, in particular with the accession to power of the

Franklin Roosevelt administration in 1934, the U.S. government acted aggressively on this premise.

If the 1930s as a whole were catastrophic, in the construction industry 1933 marked the nadir. In Calgary, the value of residential building permits for 1929 alone was greater than for the entire decade of the 1930s. Nationally, contracts for residential construction fell precipitously from $139 million in 1928 to an all-time low of $24 million in 1933. It was during the next two years that the Canadian government began to think seriously about housing and urban development. In principle, it might have considered at least four methods of reviving the building industry and of reforming the process of suburban development. In the end, the one that promoted the growth of corporate influence in house building and finance was strongly favoured. A brief consideration of the alternatives, however, serves to highlight the contingent character of the form of suburban development that emerged after 1945.

The Roads Less Travelled

The Depression called into question the stability and the rationality of the economic system, including the established methods of land development and home building. A growing number of observers argued for radical alternatives, and their favoured one was public housing, that is, housing built and owned by an agency of the state and rented, usually at subsidized rates, to low- and moderate-income households. There were obvious precedents. After the First World War, a number of European countries, notably Great Britain, had embarked on ambitious public housing programs. They served needy families, created jobs, and, through the deployment of long-term contracts, fostered the growth of large and efficient builders. In the United States, the public housing lobby collected support not only from those on the left of the political spectrum, such as the housing reformer Catherine Bauer, but also from conservative builders. In 1935 the U.S. government enacted legislation that offered federal finance to local housing projects, and soon thousands of units were built. In Canada, the construction industry was poorly organized, the public housing lobby was weaker, and federal policy was shaped by W.C. Clark, the conservative deputy minister of finance. No public housing legislation was passed until 1949. Even then the terms were ungenerous, so that provinces and municipalities were reluctant to initiate projects until they were relaxed in 1964. In the late 1960s there was a short, vigorous flurry of public housing contruction, which soon aroused opposition because it proved costly and projects were poorly designed, entailing the demolition of existing structures and the displacement of previous residents. Instead of being improved or redesigned, the program was effectively halted in 1969. In other spheres of social policy, Canadian governments have proved to be more progressive than those of their southern neighbour, but not in terms of public housing.

A second possibility was for government to assist housing cooperatives. In continental Europe, especially in Scandinavia, co-ops had a long history and by the 1930s were a strong presence. There were two types. The most common were the continuing co-ops, run democratically by their membership, which arranged for construction and then retained ownership. They charged both a membership fee (usually refundable upon departure) and a regular fee to cover heating, maintenance, and other services. In contrast, the rarer building co-ops were more temporary organizations, whose purpose was simply to build, usually through an exchange of labour, as members worked on each other's houses. Once a project was completed, however, ownership of the individual units reverted to each household. Philosophically, these two types of co-op were similar in that they were partial alternatives to the profit system. They removed portions of the building process from the private sector; they involved cooperation among households, and by limiting the opportunity for profit they made housing more affordable. In principle, the two types of cooperation could be combined in a single project. In practice, this rarely happened. As Gail Radford has shown, during the interwar years a few multi-unit projects were built in the United States. Developed under the auspices of labour unions, they were quite large. After 1945 many smaller projects were begun by Second World War veterans. Despite strong lobbying, however, the U.S. government did not pass legislation that favoured these organizations until 1949, and even then only in the face of opposition from the real estate industry. The co-op lobby in Canada was weaker, and federal interest in co-ops remained lukewarm until the 1970s, when they were recognized as an alternative to public housing.

From the 1930s until the 1970s the only government programs to favour co-ops were those developed at the provincial level. The seed was planted in Tompkinsville, Nova Scotia. In that province during the 1930s a strong cooperative movement had developed in association with the Extension Department of the Catholic University, St Francis Xavier. Its activities were confined to farming, the fishery, and the establishment of small credit institutions, when Mary Arnold, an organizer from New York City, happened to pay a summer visit to the village of Reserve Mines in Cape Breton. With a small group of miners she developed the idea of applying for financial assistance to the Nova Scotia Housing Commission. This commission had been established in 1934 to provide credit to employers or entrepreneurs who were interested in building low-cost housing. It had not received any takers, and the province was persuaded by Arnold to revise its terms of reference to include the possibility of providing funds to co-ops. The scheme that evolved was that of a building co-op, with members exchanging labour and eventually acquiring their own houses.

Tompkinsville was a great success and was heralded not

only in Canada but also in the United States. Favourable reports were published in *Maclean's* and *Reader's Digest*, and the scheme was even given grudging support in *Canadian Business*, where one writer commented, 'it all adds up to a better standard of living in the only way possible, by hard work, not by hard talking.' Politically, co-ops were acceptable to a wider range of opinion than public housing. The early projects were in mining communities but, as I have recently shown, after 1945 small building co-ops sprang up across the province, including the suburbs of the larger cities, and they involved a wide range of people. Under these auspices, 5,475 dwelling units were built in Nova Scotia before the program was shut down in 1972. By the 1960s their success was signalled by federal involvement in a large land-assembly project at Sackville, New Brunswick. By then, the commission scheme had been copied elsewhere in the Atlantic region, and building co-ops also sprang up in Quebec, Ontario, and the western provinces. Quebec, especially, developed a strong movement, which was associated with the Catholic Church and the League of Catholic Workers. By 1960 building co-ops were responsible for the construction of about 6,000 dwellings. Many of the local groups hired contractors rather than investing sweat equity, and it is likely that they derived at least some of their inspiration from European precedents. Certainly, the Garden City influence was strong in places like St-Léonard and the Cité-Jardin du Tricentenaire. In Quebec, however, as elsewhere, they were part of a grass-roots movement that received little assistance, or even acknowledgment, from the federal government. In 1944, under the direction of C.A. Curtis of Queen's University, a report on housing and community development was prepared for the federal Advisory Committee on Reconstruction. Appendix E of this report dealt with cooperative housing. Committee members praised the Nova Scotia plan as a model but in the main body of the report favoured public rental projects, and for many years the federal government paid little attention to the co-op option. In the 1970s it eventually offered support to the continuing co-ops, but not to the building co-ops pioneered in Nova Scotia.

Apart from public housing and cooperatives, a third option for the federal government to get involved was to provide housing and revive construction by helping families to build their own houses. Aided self-help, as this type of program came to be known in the late 1940s, had evolved in western Europe during the interwar years. The most effective and sustained program was that developed after 1927 by the city of Stockholm: the municipality laid out subdivisions and then provided finance, prefabricated building materials, and on-site instruction to successful applicants. The program ran continuously through the 1930s and into the post-war period and was widely regarded – in Britain, the United States, and Australia – as a huge success. It was a very inexpensive means of housing moderate-income families and of creating demand for building materials. During the 1930s and 1940s writers for *Maclean's*, *Saturday Night*, and other magazines argued that the federal government should emulate, or at least adapt, this model to Canadian circumstances. It also was endorsed by the Curtis Report, but to no avail. No such program was deliberately adopted by any government in Canada. In fact, however, after 1945 a program that contained several elements of the Stockholm plan did evolve surreptitiously.

Even before the tide of war in Europe had turned against Germany, the federal government began to plan for the readjustment of veterans to civilian life. It sought to avoid the distress and unrest that had followed the First World War, and it eventually fashioned the comprehensive and comparatively generous Veterans Charter, which eased the rehabilitation of veterans in a variety of ways. One of its main elements was the Veterans' Land Act (1942), whose purpose was to facilitate the (re)settlement of veterans on the land. This act included a provision for part-time farming on plots as small as two acres (and occasionally smaller). The idea was to enable workers in urban industry to supplement their wages and to provide them with a means to obtain a modest subsistence if the economy turned sour. Many veterans seized upon this option as a way of acquiring suburban homes, of which there was a severe shortage until the mid-1950s. By stealth, they made the small-holdings scheme into an urban housing program, and it became the most popular element of the Veterans' Land Act.

Those who framed the Land Act had not given much thought as to how those buildings might be constructed. In 1945–6 the Department of Veterans Affairs, which administered the act, was prevailed upon to develop a subdivision program using the limited amount of land that it had acquired for post-war settlement. Scattered across the country, these twenty-six subdivisions were innovatively planned, and houses were erected by professional builders. Unfortunately, cost overruns and botched workmanship created a scandal. The Veterans' Land Administration made no more efforts to create whole subdivisions and instead encouraged veterans to make their own arrangements for house construction, preferably on widely scattered sites. Although the agency had assumed that veterans would hire contractors, few could afford to do so. Instead, a growing majority sought approval to do the work themselves. At first the administration discouraged the practice, but as owner-builders proved that they were capable of doing good work – better, as administrators eventually conceded, than the so-called professionals – a new arrangement was worked out. In 1949 a 'Build Your Own Home' scheme was launched. The administration provided financing in stages, courses of instruction in house planning and construction, advice in the purchase of materials, and, most important, on-site instruction and assistance.

The scheme proved very popular, with demand outstripping expectations, in large part because it was well run. As Tricia Shulist and I have shown from interviews that we

11   House building in suburban Windsor, Ontario. Under the Veterans' Land Act, veterans such as B.E. Strauth obtained finance and technical assistance to build their own homes. This successful housing program was not made available to Canadians in general. (G. Hunter / National Archives of Canada / PA-197738)

conducted in the Hamilton area, veterans had nothing but praise for the program. One claimed that it was 'the best thing that the government ever did for veterans' while another, more cynical, offered the backhanded compliment that it was 'one of the few government plans that really worked.' It was also praised by a range of politicians, not just those in the governing party. One of its more persistent enthusiasts was Herbert Herridge, CCF member for the Kootenays, who in 1955 declared it to be 'the best housing legislation we have in Canada.' The irony is that it was intended to be a land settlement scheme, not a housing program, and it has not usually been regarded as such by scholars. By the time the program ended in 1975, the Department of Veterans Affairs had helped almost 50,000 families to acquire houses in this manner, making homes for perhaps 250,000 people. Many would not otherwise have been able to afford a house of their own, or at least not for many years.

The inadvertent successes of the Nova Scotia building co-ops and of the Veterans' Land Act serve to highlight the latent demand for approaches to house building that tapped community-based skills and initiatives. The lessons were ignored. Despite these initiatives and despite the U.S. example of public housing during the 1930s, when the federal government began to take the issue of urban development seriously after 1935, it proceeded on an entirely different path.

Creating Corporate Finance

While the Canadian government found no inspiration in the public housing program of the United States, it did choose to adapt the model of the U.S. Federal Housing Administration (FHA). Established in 1934, the FHA was supposed to revive the housing industry by promoting efficiency and by revolutionizing the system of mortgage finance. Instead of short-term 'balloon' mortgages, the FHA insisted that 'approved' lenders must offer long-term amortization. To encourage lenders to seek approval, it offered government-backed mortgage insurance so that lenders were protected in the event of default. This induced the cooperation of most lending institutions, except the savings and loans companies, which developed similar lending practices but independently of the FHA.

The Canadian government chose to copy the FHA. Under the Dominion Housing Act of 1935 (DHA), approved lenders were encouraged to provide long-term, amortized mortgages with DHA insurance. This arrangement favoured the established lending institutions; for only they were able to secure the approval of the federal office that administered the DHA. By implication, it challenged the dense network of local mortgage brokers and individual lenders that had hitherto been responsible for the majority of residential mortgages in most Canadian cities. In promoting a more corporate system, however, the Canadian government had to work harder than its U.S. counterpart. Institutional finance was in short supply, since banks were not involved in the mortgage market. In order to encourage other institutions to participate, the federal government found it necessary to provide funds. It did so through the mechanism of the 'joint loan': those who obtained DHA mortgages received three-quarters of their financing from the lending institution and one-quarter from the government.

Even with the encouragement of joint loans, the impact of the DHA was more limited than that of the FHA. Almost the only lending institutions to seek approval as DHA lenders were the insurance companies, and they preferred to lend on the better houses in the higher-class suburbs. As John Belec has shown, between 1935 and 1938 a disproportionate number of DHA recipients were affluent. In Toronto, managers and professionals made up only 7.4 per cent of all household heads but 41 per cent of all recipients of DHA loans. Virtually all loans in the Toronto area went into a handful of select suburbs: North Toronto, Forest Hill, and Kingsway Park. In some cities, notably Hamilton and Vancouver, the program reached a wider range of people, but everywhere it was quite exclusive.

Mortgage finance remained the cornerstone of federal housing policy into the post-war period. In 1938 the National Housing Act (NHA) replaced the original DHA, assimilating its main provisions. Until 1945 this was the responsibility of a division within the Ministry of Finance, which reflected its businesslike outlook. Effective in 1946, the administration of all housing programs (except for the Veterans' Land Act) was transferred to a new Crown corporation, the Central (now Canada) Mortgage and Housing Corporation (CMHC). The chief inspector of mortgages at Sun Life, Canada's largest insurance company, was appointed as its first president. Humphrey Carver, a British-born planner who worked in various capacities for CMHC from the late 1940s to the 1960s, recalls that the perfect mortgage was the 'Holy Grail' of CMHC's president, David Mansur. The name of the new agency underlined its corporate outlook and the dominance of finance in its operations. Subsequent revisions to the NHA and to the mandate of CMHC served to emphasize this position further. The most important were made in 1954, when the system of joint loans was replaced by a straightforward insurance arrangement modelled on the FHA. Simultaneous revisions to the Bank Act allowed the chartered banks to enter the mortgage field for the first time in three-quarters of a century. In this manner the federal government worked to marry suburban development with corporate finance.

Promoting the Corporate Suburb

The system of mortgage finance that CMHC became responsible for promoting could take effect only when it was linked to new methods of construction and land subdivision. Housing experts agreed that the building industry was backward and inefficient, and that to modernize it governments would have to promote large companies. The federal government took steps in this direction during the early 1940s. By 1941 unemployment in most urban areas had dropped almost to zero as men entered the armed forces and as the wartime economy boomed. A housing shortage soon emerged, especially in centres of wartime production, as people migrated from rural areas in order to find work. To relieve the shortage, Wartime Housing, a Crown corporation, was established under the direction of Joseph Pigott, a prominent Hamilton contractor. Wartime

12   Model home display, Eaton's, Calgary, 1948. Canada Mortgage and Housing Corporation sponsored national competitions to generate designs for houses that would meet NHA guidelines. Department stores and lumber dealers featured these and other models in order to boost sales. By the late 1940s boxy designs were giving way to modest ranch-style bungalows. (Provincial Archives of Alberta. BL 1441)

Housing built about 25,000 dwellings in urban centres across the country from Halifax to North Vancouver. Since only a handful of basic designs were used, they became the first truly national type of housing. In letting construction contracts, Pigott nurtured local builders that had growth potential. Within the scope of a short-lived program, however, he could achieve only modest success.

Attempts to modernize the building industry took a different form after 1945. Wartime Housing continued operations for a short time, building for veterans, but after being assimilated by CMHC, it was wound down. Most of its rental stock was sold, usually to existing tenants at favourable prices. CMHC looked for other ways to provide builders with a secure market in which to grow and invest. Like the American FHA, the federal government had been developing subdivision and building guidelines since the 1930s. These guidelines specified minimum standards in the provision of basic services, in street widths, preferred layouts, dwelling setbacks, building materials, structural performance, and so forth. Houses and neighbourhoods that did not conform could not qualify for NHA insurance and so were avoided by most institutional mortgage lenders. The purpose was to establish 'NHA' houses as a basic standard. After 1946 CMHC developed the Integrated Housing Plan, under which speculative builders would agree to sell NHA-financed houses at a price previously agreed upon, while CMHC undertook to buy back unsold houses. In the late 1940s about half of all NHA-insured houses were being erected under this plan. In 1954 the agency began to employ its own inspectors. In this manner, step by step, it promoted the emergence of the corporate subdivision. Conforming to agency guidelines on street layout and construction standards, produced on a large scale by cost-efficient methods and financed by approved corporate lenders, the packaged suburb was the government's vision of the suburban future.

Provincial and Local Initiatives in the 1940s and 1950s

Slowly, provincial and municipal governments followed the federal lead in taking more control over the process of suburban development. The most significant developments occurred within the decade after 1945.

In the Curtis Report of 1944 recommendations were made regarding the importance of community planning, and in the early post-war years a number of provinces revised their planning acts. In Alberta, relevant legislation was revised several times in the late 1940s, and new planning acts were passed in 1950 and again in 1953. The most important changes, however, were made in Ontario, where the planning act of 1946 extended, consolidated, and rationalized the whole system. The Ministry of Planning and Development was given the power to turn down those subdivision proposals that it deemed premature – too far ahead of demand – or lacking in basic services. Municipalities were required to prepare 'official plans,' a cornerstone of which was a comprehensive zoning scheme. In Canada and the United States, zoning – that is, the designation of specific areas for particular types of land use – had originated in the early years of the century. Typically, zoning developed in an ad hoc fashion in response to petitions from local property owners. (Tenants carried little weight, since they did not have the municipal franchise at that time.) In Toronto, Peter Moore has documented the steady growth of zoning-like restrictions that prohibited non-residential uses from residential areas, along with more specific prohibitions against apartment houses in areas of single-family houses. These restrictions accumulated until, by mid-century, they covered much of the city. In Vancouver, a broader zoning initiative emerged in the 1920s. As John Weaver has shown, it was supported by real estate interests, which saw municipal zoning as a useful extension of the private deed restrictions that were already helping to guarantee property values in the more desirable neighbourhoods. In general, however, it was only in the late 1940s that zoning was made into a systematic planning tool and widely applied in newly developing suburbs. In Ontario, only one municipality had an official plan by 1946, and one other had a comprehensive zoning by-law. Within a decade these numbers had jumped to fifty-seven and forty-eight, respectively. After a long period in which patterns of land use at the suburban fringe had been determined largely by the hopes and expectations of land developers, they were increasingly being brought under the control of local planning boards and municipalities.

The rise of zoning and its integration into the planning system had two important consequences. The first was to systematize a rigid separation of land uses and on a large scale. Land economists and planners justified zoning in terms of externalities, which are the uncompensated costs (and benefits) produced by the users of specific parcels of land. The classic example is the polluting factory, which imposes costs on its neighbours, especially those downwind. It makes sense to keep such activity away from residential areas where air, noise, and water-borne pollution will have the most detrimental effects. After 1945 this thinking was taken to an extreme, being used to justify the segregation of houses, even from the stores to which families might need daily access. As John Sewell and Edward Relph have shown, zoning became part of a modernizing vision that sought to create a tidy, rational, planned environment. Planners recognized that suburbs would contain all types of land use, but they believed that each should have its own place. Separating houses, offices, and industry, they also stripped residential areas of anything other than dwellings, schools, and the occasional church, compelling residents to do even convenience shopping by car.

These newly homogeneous housing areas were designed as 'neighbourhood units.' This was the appropriately generic term coined by the U.S. planner Clarence Perry in 1929 to define and designate a particular scale of residential development. Perry's idea was that each unit should focus on an elementary school and be bounded by major arterial roads. Given the prevailing family size of the early post-war years, this translated into a population of 5–6,000, or about 1,500 dwellings. This child- and family-centred concept seemed tailor made for the suburbs, where planners and developers soon made it the norm after 1945.

Changes in federal and provincial legislation slowly filtered to the level of the suburban municipality. Provinces
had the constitutional power to compel municipalities to
act as they saw fit. They could abolish or amalgamate local
governments where they perceived that either course was
in the public interest. In 1953 Ontario created a government for Metropolitan Toronto, in part as a response to
the problems of unregulated development that had been
occurring for decades. This process entailed the transfer of
some municipal functions from area municipalities and
radically changed the planning environment within which
large parts of Toronto's post-war suburbs evolved.

Federal initiatives were felt indirectly. The subdivision
and building guidelines for NHA housing gave municipalities the incentive to enact or revise building regulations;
without them they could not attract NHA builders and lenders. At the same time, after 1945, when there was a huge
housing demand but when most families could afford only
a basic dwelling, they knew that regulations should reflect
current technology. At that time most regulations specified
particular materials – as opposed to requiring certain levels
of performance – and they rapidly became outdated. As
John Smith and Bruce MacKinnon note in a piece for
Maclean's in 1947, at a time when cheap wallboard was
becoming available, the City of Toronto still required interior walls to be plastered 'three coats at union rates.' Montreal insisted that foundations be of poured concrete, not
concrete blocks, even though the latter had been satisfacto-
rily used elsewhere for several decades. Such requirements
added unnecessary costs, deterring both builders and buyers, who might then go elsewhere. The difficulty was that
building regulations were typically complex and interrelated: block basements made sense for certain types of construction but not for others. Individual municipalities
lacked the time and expertise to revise regulations thor-
oughly even once, and certainly not on a continuing basis.
Many were receptive to the idea of a national building code.

Soon after the Dominion Housing Act was passed, the need for a national standard became apparent, and the National Research Council was asked to draw one up. After extensive consultation, the first national building code was published in 1941. By 1950 almost 200 municipalities had adopted it, in either the full or the abridged version. In 1953 the code was updated, and by 1957 about 40 per cent of the 900 municipalities in the country had adopted it. Because adoption rates were highest among the larger municipalities, the code covered areas that were occupied by a clear majority of the Canadian population. Still, in many areas change came slowly, even on the fringes of some of the larger urban areas. In Nepean, for example, some building regulations had been introduced in 1921, but it was only in 1939 that a comprehensive by-law was passed and a system of permits instituted. In the suburbs of Kitchener, Ontario, Waterloo Township did not enact a building by-law until 1950.

It was one thing for municipalities to pass a by-law and quite another for them to enforce it. Bruce Elliott comments that, in Nepean, enforcement in the early years was 'problematic,' and the same was true in York Township during the 1920s and in North York in the late 1940s. At a time when so many new houses were being built, many suburban municipalities could not afford to employ enough inspectors to do a thorough job. Then again, because the housing shortage was so severe, inspectors often turned a blind eye to infractions. Slowly but surely, however, in one municipality after another, the standardizing effects of the national code were felt.

Conclusion

In Canada, federal housing initiatives from the 1930s onward were a weak imitation of their U.S. counterparts. The sweeping powers of the Home Owners' Loan Corporation (HOLC), which at one point had refinanced one-sixth of the entire residential mortgage debt of the United States, and the initiatives of the U.S. Public Housing Authority had no Canadian parallels. Even when judged relative to the much smaller Canadian population, the DHA had less impact than the FHA. In one way, however, the Canadian legislation mattered more. On the eve of the Great Depression, Canada did not have as significant or diversified a network of institutional mortgage lenders as did the United States. In order to establish a modern system of institutional mortgage finance, the Canadian government had to work hard. It had to drag lenders – first the insurance companies and then the banks – kicking and screaming into the modern era of mortgage finance. In the process it defined a new corporate model for Canadian suburbs. Slowly but surely, this model was buttressed by new provincial planning legislation and shaped the actions of municipalities. As builders and developers took their cue, and as consumers bought into it in unprecedented numbers, this model came to define the Canadian suburb in the post-war era.

6

The Rise of the Corporate Suburb, 1945–1960

Many people assume that suburbanization began after the Second World War. Their mistake is understandable. In 1945, after a decade of the Great Depression and six years of war, there was a huge backlog of demand for housing. Young men and women had postponed marriage, young couples had postponed having children, and older families with children had waited to trade up to larger houses. In the prosperity of the post-war economy, these families were soon in the market for a house. During the 1930s and early 1940s the annual production of housing units never rose above 50,000, except briefly in 1940–1. In the late 1940s the rate climbed rapidly, reaching 90,000 in 1948, falling back with the onset of the Korean War in 1951, but topping 100,000 in 1953 and rising thereafter until the end of the decade. The great majority of these houses were built at the urban fringe, and, because most cities were no longer interested in annexation, they lay in areas controlled by suburban municipalities. The suburbs mushroomed.

In numbers, the scale of the post-war suburban boom was not much different from that of the Laurier years, but it occupied much more space. In 1910 almost everyone walked or took the streetcar to work; by 1960 the majority drove automobiles. In 1945 there were just over 1.1 million cars registered in Canada; by 1952 the number had doubled and then redoubled within less than a decade, reaching 4.3 million by 1961. The automobile allowed men, especially, to live much further from work and encouraged suburbs to spread at lower densities. Instead of twenty-five-foot lots, forty- and fifty-foot lots became the norm, larger still around smaller cities and in affluent suburbs. The sprawl of settlement was even greater than the growth in lot size might suggest. Private cars required a much more extensive infrastructure of roads and parking lots. In the interwar years, stores retreated from the street as developers accommodated cars with angle parking. In the 1950s the retreat became a rout as on-street parking morphed into storefront parkettes, then into larger lots, and finally into the oceans of space that surrounded the new stand-alone malls. The first retail malls, built in the early 1950s, allowed more space for parking than for retail floor space. In its geographical extent, then, the post-war suburban boom was wholly unprecedented. Because they were built around the automobile, and even though the architecture of that era was distinctive, the developments of the early post-war years are immediately recognizable as suburban in a way that those of the Laurier boom are not.

It was also in this period that Canadian suburbs first became stereotyped. It would not have occurred to writers in the 1900s to speak in generic terms about the suburbs. In Toronto in 1913 there were unplanned fringe areas like Earlscourt and affluent subdivisions like Lawrence Park, with gradations between, but there was no such thing as a standard suburb. The situation remained the same during the 1920s, although by then some diversity was being ironed out. By the 1940s, however, people spoke freely about 'the suburbs' in general and indeed about 'suburbia,' a generic and pejorative term, which had been coined in London, England, in the late nineteenth century but which gained currency in Canada only after the Second World War. Its first significant appearance in the *Globe and Mail*, for example, was in an editorial on 11 July 1946. Entitled 'Standardized – Like Anthills,' the writer damned Toronto's 'endless

13   Park Royal, West Vancouver, 1962. The first suburban shopping
centre to be anchored by two department stores, Park Royal heralded a
new shopping experience as well as a new type of suburban landscape.
(West Vancouver Municipal Archives, aerial photograph by Eric Cable,
1960)

dwellings of suburbia, each meticulously exact on its thirty-
seven foot frontage, not an inch out of line.' This was new.
When Humphrey Carver grumbled about 'uniformity,
conformity,' and Norman Pearson attacked the 'identical
houses on standard lots in featureless neighbourhooods,'
they implied not only that things could have been done differently but that, until quite recently, they had been.

The *Globe and Mail* editorial writer, like most observers,
overstated the case. After 1945 everything was not suddenly
different. When immigration resumed after 1945, Italians,
Jews, and other minorities continued to make their way into
suburban ethnic enclaves. So, too, did many workers. For a
short time, suburbs were still made in a variety of ways and

were occupied by a variety of people. But from the very beginning there was less class diversity in the suburbs than before 1939, and it was soon to be reduced further. Between 1945 and about 1960 it is possible to trace the rise of a corporate, packaged suburb that was designed, financed, and built in an increasingly standard way. This product, and the debt-encumbered style of life that it embodied, did not emerge overnight. There is a story to be told.

Promoting the Corporate Suburb

Like its U.S. counterpart, the Canadian government was eager to promote suburban development after 1945. Suburban homes satisfied real needs. They also created an abundant demand for a wide range of consumer goods and eventually played a significant role in sustaining the long post-war economic boom. In the United States the Federal Housing Administration (FHA) has often been criticized for favouring suburbs over cities, thereby contributing to the process of suburban sprawl at the expense of inner city decline. The FHA did not finance many city houses, because they often failed to meet the agency's construction or subdivision guidelines. Then, too, as Kenneth Jackson has shown, it encouraged lenders to avoid, or 'redline,' inner city areas whose decline was seen to be inevitable and where real estate investments were thought to be too risky. The FHA was especially wary of African-American districts or adjacent areas that were likely to experience what was known as racial transition. Although it is impossible to determine the total effect of such FHA policies, it is clear that they not only encouraged development in the suburbs but also encouraged disinvestment in the central cities.

In some ways, Canadian legislation discriminated even more sharply in favour of the suburbs. During the debates that led to the passage of the Dominion Housing Act (DHA) in 1935, some references were made to the needs of low-income Canadians, but the main purpose of the act was to revive the building industry. For that reason, DHA (and later National Housing Act – NHA) financing was made available only on new housing. Since only a few houses could be built in existing neighbourhoods, and even then on scattered sites that might not meet agency guidelines, the suburban bias of the DHA/NHA was almost complete. It does not seem that the federal government encouraged lenders to redline inner city areas, and the issue of race was not a significant factor. Implicitly, however, federal policy encouraged lenders and investors to favour the suburbs and particular suburban residents. Federal housing policy also favoured a particular type of suburban development, one in which corporate finance would underpin the growth of large land developers and builders that could fashion fully packaged suburbs. In the end they were successful in achieving most aspects of this goal, but not all of them.

Mortgage Finance

Slowly, federal housing legislation helped to make institutional lenders dominant in the market for mortgages on new houses. This trend cannot be traced through published sources, but Doris Forrester and I have documented it for Hamilton. Using property assessment and land registry records for this city, we gathered mortgage information on a large sample of single-family dwellings for 1931, 1941, and 1951. For properties in each year we determined which had been built within the previous decade, thereby allowing us to distinguish 'new' from 'old' houses. Before the federal government became involved in the mortgage market, lending institutions played a minor role in the financing of new houses. Among the Hamilton residences that were mortgaged in 1931 and that had been built in the previous decade only 18 per cent were financed by lending institutions, these being an equal mixture of insurance and trust as well as building and loans companies. The remainder were financed by private individuals. By 1941 the impact of the DHA was very apparent: the share of the market held by lending institutions had more than doubled, to 44 per cent, and among these lending institutions the insurance companies, virtually the only ones to participate in DHA financing, were now overwhelmingly dominant. This new pattern of finance was maintained during the 1940s, when, because of a rapid increase in the level of construction, it began to have a significant impact.

The growing penetration of institutions, especially insurance companies, into the mortgage market was most apparent in the suburbs. During the late 1940s a significant amount of new construction occurred in older areas, including suburban districts whose development had almost ceased after 1929. Lending institutions showed little interest in such areas. Instead, they channelled their money into new subdivisions. In Hamilton they were concentrated in the Bartonville area, in west Hamilton, and on the Mountain, an extensive area above the Niagara escarpment that had recently been opened up for more extensive development by the widening of a road access route. In these areas in the late 1940s lending institutions provided about three-quarters of the mortgages on new homes. Even as early as 1951 federal legislation already had played a large part in establishing a new norm of corporate finance in such suburbs.

For some years, however, the influence of the lending institutions remained very uneven. During the 1930s there were extensive areas of the country where 'approved' lenders were inactive. The most obvious problem arose in 'remote areas,' where lenders did not have offices or representatives. Since this problem persisted into the 1940s, when the Central (now Canada) Mortgage and Housing Corporation (CMHC) was established in 1946, it was given the authority to make 'direct loans' in such districts: on these loans the Crown agency was responsible for the full amount. But this problem was not confined to remote areas. From the very beginning, politicians had com-

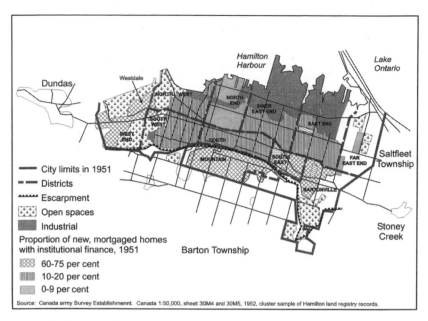

14   Institutional mortgage finance in Hamilton, 1951. Directed by
Canada Mortgage and Housing Corporation, lending institutions channelled funds into some suburbs while ignoring others. By the end of the
decade, through planning controls and a national building code, lenders were encouraged to be active everywhere, helping to create the standard corporate suburb. (Richard Harris)

plained that lenders were reluctant to make loans in many
suburban districts, chiefly those occupied by lower-income
households. While he was still with Sun Life, in 1936 David
Mansur commented that in Montreal 'entire working-class
communities were regarded as "undesirable districts" for
mortgage lending.' His own company was concentrating its
activity in Westmount and Mount Royal, while neglecting
the city's East End.

Such discrimination on economic grounds was later reinforced by CMHC policy, which generally withheld NHA
financing from subdivisions that lacked basic services,
including piped water and sewers. Insurers listened. In a

piece that he wrote for the *Residential Appraiser* W.B. McCutcheon, the Manitoba regional manager for Manufacturers Life, advised appraisers and lenders to exercise 'unusual vigilance' in unserviced suburbs, which many might have taken as advice to 'redline.' Complaints about the lack of finance in less desirable suburbs resurfaced in the late 1940s and early 1950s. Apparently, less desirable suburbs included Burnaby (east of Vancouver), York and East York townships (north of Toronto), most of Ottawa's suburbs, almost all of those of Edmonton, and extensive districts in Montreal, including the East End and the south shore. In Hamilton, registry data show that institutions made virtually no loans in the eastern suburbs that stretched into Saltfleet Township. In terms of the availability of corporate finance, for a time the situation seems to have been one of feast or famine, with little in between.

The mortgage famine encouraged a number of politicians to press CMHC to make direct loans available in targeted suburbs as well as in remote areas. With the encouragement of suburban constituents, they pressed hard on this issue, but the agency resisted on the grounds that lenders should be active in these areas and that one day they would be. For several years those who settled in many of Canada's post-war suburbs were compelled to seek mortgage funds from private individuals, as their predecessors in the interwar period had done, or to manage without. In time the problem was overcome and, judging from the parliamentary debates, was fading from memory by the end of the 1950s. Undoubtedly, the entry of the banks onto the mortgage scene in 1954 had some impact. Even more important, however, were rapid changes in the process of land development.

Land Development

In the decade or so after 1945 the growth of corporate finance went hand in hand with a rapid and progressive change in the process of land development. In part, this conjunction was driven by CMHC's introduction of subdivision regulations for NHA homes; for these controls favoured integrated developments that required a large scale of operation and a line of credit that virtually mandated corporate backing. Of critical importance, however, was the rapid adoption by many municipalities of a new policy on the provision of services. Throughout the first half of the twentieth century the norm had been for municipalities to provide all services, simultaneously with house building in middle-class areas or after a delay of a few years in lower-income districts. This approach was costly, and after the First World War it had deterred most urban municipalities from annexing districts where unserviced development had occurred. The solution, worked out most dramatically in Don Mills, was for suburban developers to assume the costs, and increasingly the responsibility, for services. Developers then incorporated the costs of service provision into the price of lots or, if they also undertook to build, of finished houses.

Don Mills has often been held up as the model of the post-war corporate suburb. Between 1947 and 1952 the financier E.P. Taylor acquired 2,063 acres in the Township of North York. He commissioned a subdivision plan that, drawing upon ideas that were advanced for their day, carved the territory into quadrants in which curvilinear streets and culs-de-sac were used to define distinct neighbourhoods. Taylor's company zoned the land and imposed tight building restrictions. On his personal whim, for example, blue shingles were prohibited. Because these private regulations were stricter than those of the township, they defined the character of the area. The scale of the development was striking, but it was the servicing package that was the most innovative element of the plan. The Township of North York was unable to provide the necessary services as quickly as Taylor wished, so he himself agreed to take responsibility. Indeed, because of the size of the scheme, he even helped to pay for a major new municipal sewage treatment plant. Some important elements of this project proved to be exceptional. The zoning plan accommodated not only a shopping centre but an industrial park. Later, land subdivision projects were more likely to include at most two major types of land use. Then again, more than half of the 8,121 dwelling units that eventually were built in Don Mills were relatively affordable townhouses or apartments, whereas single-family homes were dominant in other suburbs. Private building restrictions, prominent in Don Mills, soon became unnecessary as suburban municipalities adopted and enforced their own regulations. (In very recent years, however, there has been a resurgence of private controls, especially in the more exclusive subdivisions.) Don Mills was not the first large developer-controlled subdivision. Hamilton's Westdale, which eventually contained 1,700 dwellings, was a precursor. Don Mills was not even the first planned suburb in which the developer provided services. Nevertheless, it has generally been regarded as the first major example of a new suburban type, the fully planned corporate suburb.

Other municipalities soon came to appreciate the financial advantages of passing on the costs of servicing to the developers, so much so that by the end of the 1950s this approach was the norm. For example, Michael Doucet and John Weaver report that in 1956 the City of Hamilton charged the Grisenthwaite company almost $1,500 per lot for streets and local improvements. In the following year the city began to require developers themselves to actually undertake the work. These changes mattered because, on average, improvements alone cost twice as much as the unimproved land. Previously, a land subdivider had required little capital and only very short-term credit, especially if he converted acreages into building lots very quickly. Turning subdividers into developers, the new servicing requirements changed the financial rules of the game. It was either impossible or uneconomic for developers to trouble

15   The post-war suburb, Lethbridge, Alberta, 1951. Curvilinear streets and culs-de-sac were meant to slow traffic and break monotony. Designed on the neighbourhood unit concept, clusters of about 1,500 houses were anchored by elementary schools (left foreground). Multiple versions were built by larger developers around the larger cities. (Glenbow Archives, NA 5327-293)

themselves with small subdivisions, since they now had to make substantial investments in infrastructure. To play this game they needed deep pockets or financial backing. The situation had changed from the early part of the century, when land subdividers were more often than not individuals looking for a quick profit.

The scale effects were apparent everywhere. In every major urban centre in the 1950s land developers that were producing integrated developments on a new scale were emerging. Only a few rivalled Taylor in the scale of their operations. In the mid-1950s at Pont Viau on Isle Jésus, north of Montreal island, the Riverview Investment Company planned a development of 2,200 units. They made provision for seven house models, building 250 units themselves and arranging for contractors to erect the remainder. At the same time in West Lynn Park in West Vancouver, the N.W. Hullah Construction Company laid out a subdivision of 800 units and installed services, while planning another 600-unit development in Richmond Park. In the late 1950s and early 1960s the Nu-West Group rapidly emerged as the largest builder-developer in Calgary and within a decade had expanded successfully into the Edmonton market. These developers were exceptions. More typical was M.H.N. Gruner and Company, which acquired 37 acres in Lansdowne Park, Pointe Claire, on Montreal's west island. It laid out and serviced 108 building lots on which it built three-bedroom, ranch-style houses on four basic plans. It introduced an element of variety by creating curvilinear streets and by adjusting the placement of units on each lot. On a similar scale, in Thorncliffe Heights, Calgary, the Glencoe Engineering Company planned a development of 80 units. Even these more moderate projects, described in the *Canadian Builder* (trade journal for the industry), represented a clear step up from what had been the norm.

The overall trend towards increasing scale was documented in an unpublished study of Ottawa that has been summarized by Frank Clayton. In the period 1950–4 there were 98 land developers active in the Ottawa area, half of which were responsible for the creation of fewer than 25 building lots. A decade later there were only 37 developers, and only one-quarter of them were operating on such a small scale. The increasing scale of operation meant that fewer companies came to hold an increasingly dominant position in the market. In the earlier period the four largest developers in the Ottawa area brought 30 per cent of all new lots onto the market. A decade later the share of the largest four had jumped to 53 per cent. This upward trend continued into the 1970s, by which time the growth of monopoly in the land development industry had become a major public issue. A study on land monopoly prepared for CMHC by Peter Spurr, who concluded that it had not had a major effect on house prices, nevertheless documented the corporate character of suburban development.

House Building

When in 1957 the City of Hamilton began to require subdividers to install services, a local councillor predicted that this step would finally mark the end of the small builder. This prediction made sense as long as land development and house construction went hand in hand. This convergence was what many experts and policy makers wished to make a reality. The construction industry had long been criticized for being backward. The federal government and, after 1946, CMHC did what they could to promote the growth of large builders and to integrate construction with land development. Despite some well-publicized initiatives, however, these goals generally were not met.

In the early 1950s observers in Canada and the United States viewed William Levitt's company as the model of land development and also of home building. Levitt developed three huge 'Levittowns,' one on Long Island, one outside Philadelphia, and one in New Jersey. The Long Island project alone consisted of 17,500 houses. Levitt acted both as land developer, installing all services, and as builder. His orders were so large that suppliers were willing to develop new products and to offer lower prices. He acquired many materials, including the appliances that came with his houses, through a subsidiary, North Shore Supply Company. He secured a special deal on the new thermapane windows from Libby-Owens-Ford. With Johns Manville he developed an innovative type of overlapping asbestos shingle. His business made the fortune of a small

paint company, with which he cooperated in the development of a new type of paint that could be sprayed to
impregnate sheet-rock panels to create a subtle four-tone
effect. Levitt built his own factories on site, where lumber
was precut for on-site assembly. Using time and motion
studies and resisting efforts at unionization, he developed a
fine division of labour that emphasized productivity. One
man was employed full time bolting refrigerators to floors.
For site work he scheduled teams of tradesmen, who
moved in coordinated waves across the landscape. As James
Dugan commented in *Maclean's* in 1952, this was 'the
assembly line turned inside out.' Using another metaphor
common at the time, he described Levitt as 'the Ford of
housing.'

Some Canadian developers followed this model, albeit
on a much smaller scale. A good example was G.S. Shipp.
In Toronto during the interwar years, Shipp had done custom work in several of the more prestigious suburbs,
including Kingsway Park and Forest Hill. After the war, on
the initiative of the founder's son, the company went into
mass production house building. Its first large project was
Applewood Acres in Mississauga. In a pattern that became
typical of the larger developers, it subdivided and developed Applewood in stages, at the rate of 100 units a year. It
took direct responsibility for the construction work, con-
verting a barn in the old apple orchard into a shed for storage and precutting. A feature writer in *Canadian Builder*
noted that it patterned its advertising on the American
model, building model houses and organizing a sales event
that was advertised with brochures and a light aircraft pull-
ing a sales banner. Here was the new way of doing business.

Although these methods of mass construction and sales-
manship were attempted in every Canadian city, they were
more common in Hamilton than elsewhere. In the early
1950s Hamilton was growing more rapidly than any other
major urban centre. Union jobs in the mills were well paid,
and there was huge demand for standard housing on mod-

est lots. Grisenthwaite Construction was one large company that, between 1947 and 1962, assembled land and built houses at a rate of over 100 a year. It was rivalled by E. Mills and also by Zeller Construction. Zeller had grown up in Windsor, Ontario, but by 1950 it had built hundreds of units in Ajax and Belleville and was contemplating a move to Hamilton. There it fashioned the Mount Breeze survey of 300 houses. During that summer a reporter for the *Hamilton Spectator* noted two sawmills on site and commented, 'the survey has the appearance of an outdoor factory, with crews of workers moving down the line of excavations and houses in various stages of construction.' His use of certain rhetorical tropes – the notion of the assembly line turned inside out, for example – reminds us that observers tend to see what they have learned to recognize. But clearly many companies had ambitions to operate in new ways and on a new scale.

Large builders favoured, and were favoured by, the approved corporate mortgage lenders. Builders that conformed to CMHC guidelines were able to obtain construction finance from the Crown agency and could use the availability of NHA finance as a selling point. By promoting such builders, CMHC believed that it was facilitating the construction of inexpensive housing by a newly efficient industry. By working with CMHC and the largest of the speculative, or merchant, builders, corporate lenders were able to pour money into standardized products that minimized their risk. John Bacher has estimated that by 1961, 75 per cent of all NHA-financed homes were being produced by large merchant builders.

Each of the major players had achieved its goals except, according to Humphrey Carver, those who, in buying a house, wished to express their individuality and their freedom of choice. Instead, their dwellings were 'impersonal, synthetic, exchangeable, temporary' and yielded only 'uniformity, conformity.' 'Noble motives,' Carver judged, seemed to have produced 'unexpectedly horrible results.'

We may agree with his comments about the appearance of many of the houses that were built in this era, and nowhere were they built with less imagination than in the areas of Hamilton Mountain where Grisenthwaite, Mills, and Zeller were active. However, Carver's judgment of motive seems naïve. At first, consumers were more concerned about privacy and price than with self-expression; the latter could come later. Arguably, the most important motives that built the corporate suburb were not at all those of the consumers but those of the builder and financier. Mass housing was erected by the mass builder that had ridden in on the tide of corporate finance.

Despite these well-publicized initiatives, the building industry was not remade. In 1956 the members of the Royal Commission on Canada's Economic Prospects concluded that although 'progress' had been made in construction, 'technological advances have not been nearly as spectacular as those achieved by other industries.' Of course, there were changes. In terms of house design, open-plan living and dining rooms became common, especially in the popular ranch-style bungalow. Eat-in kitchens marked a new informality in domestic life and anticipated later shifts in the domestic division of labour. Some companies experimented with plans and styles: in the late 1950s E.V. Keith in Calgary was building a new model house every month to test the marketability of innovative ideas. For the most part, they found buyers to be conservative in their tastes, perhaps because of concerns about resale value.

New materials became available after the Second World War, as manufacturers looked for fresh markets. Where permitted by building regulations, drywall soon became the norm, since it was quick, easy, and hence cheap to install. Concrete blocks also became common. Other innovations offered new methods of plumbing, wiring, siding, covering floors, heating, and cooling. They were not necessarily better, but many were cheaper, easier to use, and were progress of a sort. Dimensional lumber had already been standardized, and the same trend affected other products. Precutting was a key development, which advanced more slowly in Canada than in the United States. It was practised by the large builder-developers, including all of those mentioned above. In Lansdowne Park, for example, Gruner and Company trucked plywood and partition panels from Quebec City and made joists, rafters, and kitchen cabinets in their own shop. Frank Clayton reports that in the mid-1940s about 2,400 hours of on-site work were required to assemble the average house, but by the mid-1960s this figure had been reduced to 950 hours. Some of the reduction was accomplished by an increase in efficiency. Hand tools – above all power saws, drills, and sanders – made some types of on-site work much easier. But of at least equal importance was the transference of work from the construction site to the factory. Window and door assemblies were made off site, as were engineered roof trusses after a U.S.-based company developed new 'gang-nailing' technology. Some observers doubted that the new trusses were suitable to carry Canadian-style snow loads, and more dispersed settlement and hence construction in Canada did limit the potential for a factory-based system of production. But precutting, like other innovations, made steady and significant inroads.

One thing that changed hardly at all after 1950 was the size of the average builder. NHA builders expanded because of their participation in the federal housing program, not primarily because of any compelling logic of market competition. A recent study by Michael Buzzelli has shown that, although there have been cycles in the size structure of the building industry over the post-war period, there has been no long-term trend. Small builders – those erecting fewer than five houses a year – persisted because they remained competitive. Cheap, hand-held power tools helped them to limit the incursion of factory production into the tasks that had traditionally been undertaken on site. Tools were much cheaper than a precutting plant, an important consideration for an industry that was notoriously cyclical: an idle factory is its owner's nightmare. Then, too, the persisting diversity of building regulations was a particular handicap for the manufacturers of entirely prefabricated homes. Smith and MacKinnon cite the Faircraft house, produced in the late 1940s in the converted Fairchild Aircraft factory in Longeuil, Quebec, as an example. This manufactured house, which stood thirteen feet high, could not be erected in Longeuil itself, whose regulations (when they were enforced) required dwellings to rise at least twenty-one feet above grade. Similar regulations prohibited its installation in other Montreal suburbs, and comparable restrictions limited its use elsewhere. In Halifax, for example, a by-law required that wiring be installed on site. Such regulations crippled the nascent industry for manufactured houses. Regulations were also an irritant to traditional builders that wished to operate in more than one municipality.

Although new tools and old regulations affected the evolution of the industry, two other considerations guaranteed the persistence of the small builder. The first was the wave of immigration that gathered momentum after 1945. Of particular importance to the construction industry was the immigration of Italians. On arrival in Canada some Italians already had construction skills, especially in the use of concrete, but, more important, those who lacked such skills brought a willingness to do work that Canadian-born workers shunned. One such immigrant was Frank Colantonio, who immigrated to Canada in 1949 at the age of twenty-six. His informal apprenticeship in the construction industry began, like that of so many others among his countrymen, by digging ditches. One summer he was given the opportunity to learn the basics of rough carpentry on the job, including the use of a hammer and the new power saw. He bluffed his way into a job requiring more skilled work, hanging doors and installing baseboards, from which he graduated to kitchen cabinets. Night classes in carpentry and drafting rounded out his education in the trade. Based on his experience and observation, Colantonio comments in his autobiography that 'almost any man with a few tools and a truck could become a contractor in the house-building field.' The industry required little capital or skills, and those large developers wanting to invest in fixed factory equipment were generally undercut by the availability of an army of immigrants who worked all hours, in all conditions, and for almost any wage. As Colantonio concludes, 'the main things were a willingness to work hard and a network of contacts in your own community.'

Networks were important because workers were hired on a temporary basis through a complex web of subcontracting, the second critical feature of the industry. Subcontracting had long been common in house building. Between the wars, for example, it was used extensively by the builders active in Kingsway Park and Westdale. After 1945 the use of subcontractors was extended to include those with heavy equipment that specialized in basements, and the practice became ubiquitous. There are no exact data for the early post-war years, but a later study indicated that in 1971 60 per cent of builders subcontracted more than three-quarters of all construction work. Some builders retained a few of the better tradesmen on salary. Most hired tradesmen when they were needed, skilled trades on a project basis and labourers by the day. Subcontractors were hired through a system of bid-peddling: builders informed subcontractors what their competitors had bid. It was a cut-throat business, which did little to maintain standards, while keeping wages low and working conditions poor. It also created a level playing field for the builders, which were nominally responsible for construction. Almost all builders, large and small, used the same web of subcontracting trades. Buying in bulk, the larger builders could cut better deals on materials, but their advantage in the labour market was negligible. Indeed, to the extent that they minimized overhead by exploiting their own and their family's labour – by working punishing hours and asking their wives to keep the books and their sons to help out after school, on weekends, and during summer holidays – small builders made and kept themselves competitive.

The large builders, some of which were active in land development, mostly concentrated on the corporate suburbs, but small builders were everywhere. They did not have the capital to develop land, but they were often given a piece of the action in large subdivisions. Land developers liked to have a stable of builders to which they could direct customers, each being responsible for a particular style or size of house. More than fifty builders were eventually responsible for building houses in post-war Don Mills. The smaller builders were almost the only type to be active within the built-up areas of cities, erecting infill houses on scattered sites. It might seem that they would also have been dominant in the redlined, unserviced suburbs, but here, for about a decade after 1945, they were faced by a rival with whom they often found it impossible to compete: the amateur.

Doing It Themselves

Although it has been largely forgotten except by those involved, during the early post-war years there was a huge boom in owner-building. The only country for which data are available on this phenomenon is Australia, where between 1945 and 1955 one-third of all single-family houses were built by owners for their own use. The rate peaked in the early 1950s at more than two-fifths. Conditions in Australia, Canada, and the United States were much the same, and trade journals and popular magazines indicate that rates of owner-building in these countries were also similar. While the corporate suburb was being refined, the do-it-yourself suburb had its last hurrah.

Owner-building underwent a resurgence for a variety of reasons. First, after 1945 there was a severe shortage of skilled tradesmen. Second, because of the Depression, and with so many young families eager to buy their first houses, there was a general shortage of savings for down payments. Third, the new affordability of cars enabled people to settle further from city jobs on cheap, unserviced land. Finally, the new materials and tools that helped the small professional builder were a boon to the amateur. As the success of the Veterans' Land Act program of the 1940s proved, with patience, hard work, a little instruction, and a couple of power tools, almost anyone could build a house.

In some areas, owner-builders created shacktowns that resembled those of the early years of the century. An article in *Maclean's* illustrated part of one of the more extensive of these settlements, on Montreal's south shore. More commonly owner-builders erected solid but modest, single-storey houses, often without basements, running water, or sewer connections. Residents relied on chemical toilets or outdoor privies and drew water from wells. This sort of development characterized all of the areas that were redlined in the early 1950s. For example, Donald Wetherell and Irene Kmet have suggested that it was apparent in many Calgary suburbs, including Montgomery, Forest Lawn, Beverly, and Bowness. Some observers deplored these places as instant slums, but they were soon improved. Continuing prosperity meant that even lower-income workers soon made shacks into respectable homes. A fine example were the Sileikas, immigrants from Latvia, who settled in Weston, northwest of Toronto. The account of their early years in Canada, lightly fictionalized by the son, Antanas, tells a common story. The father dug and covered a basement, where the family lived in cramped conditions through a winter. A visiting inspector pointed out that living in a basement was not only unhealthy but contravened building regulations, but he was successfully kept at bay on the grounds that there was no alternative. The first floor was built on evenings and Saturdays – but not on the day of rest – with the help of co-workers and cousin Stan, who was paid in liquor. The family ran out of money before they had installed interior doors, but they managed to purchase one for the bathroom in time for the visit of a rich uncle from Detroit. When the house was complete, one floor was rented out, and later, as a sideline, the father turned his garage into a small factory, employing friends to assemble windows. In the end, the house passed inspection. Indeed, it was their neighbour's house, built by a contractor for a stand-offish British couple, that developed a crack in the basement. Some details in Sileika's account may be invented or adapted to suit his narrative purpose, but the spirit of the account rings true for many tens of thousands of Canadians, both new immigrants and the native born, in the early post-war years.

Another distinctive feature of owner-building after 1945 was that women played an active role. Accounts of suburban construction in the early years of the century, such as those transcribed by Bill Bailey from oral histories, suggest that in that era men did almost all the physical work of house building. Later accounts, including those of veterans who received assistance from the Veteran's Land Act, reported by Shulist and Harris, show that in the post-war years women did much of this work, as well as keeping house and often looking after young children. As Veronica Strong-Boag has observed, the women were 'as active in all weathers as their husbands.' Usually they viewed themselves simply as 'helpers,' but sometimes they did much more. A reporter for the *Hamilton Spectator*, for example, tells of a schoolteacher in Stoney Creek who built the family house during her summer holiday, her husband and friends contributing what they could on weekends. Transgressions of the usual division of labour attract attention, but such accounts were common enough to indicate that, routinely, everyone pitched in.

The surge of demand from amateur builders galvanized lumber dealers. Traditionally, dealers had located in warehouse or industrial districts where they had relied on the contractor trade. They concentrated on selling lumber and related materials, leaving hardware, tools, plumbing, and electrical supplies to the department stores or to other specialized businesses. This practice did not suit consumers, who preferred one-stop shopping in convenient locations, ideally along suburban arterial roads with generous parking. As consumer demand accelerated, progressive dealers relocated, diversified, and offered additional services. In Brantford, Ontario, Summerhayes Lumber added a home planning section and encouraged customers to use their washroom, which featured their new line in plumbing supplies. In Port Arthur (now Thunder Bay), Ontario, J.H. McLennan broadcast its new business plan by adopting the slogan 'Everything in Building Materials.' Previously, barely half of its business had come from consumers; soon, the proportion was three-quarters. Out west, the Beaver Lumber chain – known in the business as 'line yards' – made rapid headway with this new orientation. To compete with mail-order companies, which underwent a minor resurgence after 1945, dealers offered plan services and many made their own house kits. Kits were usually sold on a local basis and adapted to local tastes and needs. Seemingly, they were available almost everywhere, even, according to Gerald Pocius, in Newfoundland outports. In this manner, as dealers responded to the demand from owner-builders, they also made owner-building more viable.

The greatest adjustment that building suppliers had to make was in selling to women. Even in households where construction work was done by men, women were prominent in planning and purchasing. Accustomed to the bright showroom displays of the department and clothing stores, they were unimpressed by the dingy disorder, casual service, and sometimes unwanted personal attention to be found in the average lumber dealership. The point was made by R.C. McMillan, sales manager for Crown Zellerbach, a Vancouver-based forest and lumber company, in his standard talk to local lumbermen's associations. 'My wife wouldn't go down to the wharf,' he observed jovially, 'but she would go down to a nice area around a Supermarket where there's a beautiful retail lumber dealer shop and wander around there and spend my money freely.' Lumber dealers stood to lose business to other retail outlets, including department and hardware stores, that had more experience in serving the female customer. In 1949 it was reported in the *Prairie Lumberman* that through a regional survey of lumber yards it was found that only 15 per cent appealed to women. The writer concluded that dealers should smarten up. Soon many did so, building showrooms on suburban auto strips and transforming their outlets into all-purpose centres for the home handyman and woman.

As dealers began to cater to consumers, owner-building was drawn into the commercial mainstream. Amateur builders in the 1900s and 1910s sketched house plans on scraps of paper, scrounged materials, made their own concrete blocks, and improvised. In the early 1950s couples purchased house plans and kits that differed little from those used by many professional builders. They bought a wide range of tools and received advice on techniques, materials, styles, and furnishings from consumer magazines as well as local dealers. Dealers and, slowly, financial institutions became more willing to offer them credit. 'Do-it-yourself' (DIY), a term that was apparently coined, and was certainly popularized, by *Time* magazine in 1952 became respectable. Indeed, in the modest form of finishing the attic or basement, it became so mainstream as to be almost de rigueur. To extend their market, professional builders sold 'shell' houses that were not completely finished. By the late 1950s, as families continued to grow, even those who had purchased finished houses began to remodel, and the wave of owner-building segued into a boom in DIY. In terms of construction, the distinction between the corporate and the unserviced suburbs, once sharp, soon began to blur.

Convergence

Between the 1920s and the late 1950s the suburb-making process was both modernized and simplified. In the early twentieth century there were four types of suburbs: elite, unplanned, industrial, and middle class. By the early 1950s the application of zoning controls had virtually eliminated the industrial suburb in the traditional sense. Larger suburbs, such as York Township, routinely contained both houses and factories, not to mention retail and office centres, but without enforcing an industrial intimacy. By that time unplanned and unserviced suburbs also were under siege, as municipalities felt pressure to make land development conform to NHA guidelines or to some close approximation. This trend did not always proceed smoothly. Smaller builders, in particular, resisted the NHA and the national building code, sometimes from inertia and sometimes because they believed that their clients could not afford such standards. In 1950 Alexander Roger, reeve of Gloucester Township, reported that builders in his portion of suburban Ottawa were bridling at the building inspector's attempt to enforce a local version of the national code. They could not see why indoor plumbing was a necessity. In this resistance they were often aided and abetted by lumber dealers. In the late 1940s, for example, the Western Retail Lumberman's Association developed plans and kits for a simple house with no basement or plumbing. They wanted to do business and, unlike the policy experts in Ottawa, were content to accept prevailing community standards as to what constituted an acceptable home.

In larger numbers, amateur builders also resisted the steady encroachment of higher standards, along with their higher costs. Their opposition was most commonly stirred up when cities tried to annex unserviced suburbs. Annexation brought city services and city taxes. The drama was enacted several times around Hamilton, one of the few cities that continued to annex suburbs after 1945. Residents of Barton and Saltfleet townships organized and petitioned to keep their taxes low, taking their arguments on more than one occasion to the Ontario Municipal Board, the body that is the ultimate court of appeal on municipal issues in that province. This was a rearguard action. In the end they and their counterparts elsewhere lost their battles and ceased to fight. Municipalities adopted and enforced national building regulations. Provincial legislation compelled land developers to install services before, or while, builders were erecting houses.

Mortgage money became more readily available, on easier terms, and throughout the urban fringe. Incomes rose, and in time more people could afford the price of entry to some type of corporate, packaged development. By the end of the 1950s these developments had all but engulfed the suburbs.

7

Creeping Conformity?

Every home, every family, every person, exactly the same. Every single detail the same, except for the house numbers
Mary Ross, 'The Higher Conformity'

... migration to the suburbs revolutionizes patterns of living, buying and selling.
Richard Edsall, 'This Changing Canada'

Social commentators usually exaggerate the latest trend. At the beginning of the twentieth century, reformers painted in lurid colours the physical and moral condition of 'the slums' at a time when most slum dwellers, although poor, led respectable lives. In contrast, they idealized the healthfulness of the suburban home, which – though behind locked doors and out of earshot – contained its share of hardship, abuse, and anguish. By the 1950s new trends called for new rhetoric. Reporters and academics whipped themselves into a frenzy of criticism over suburban 'conformity.' It was not so much a trend as an accomplished fact, they claimed, and one that threatened the nation. To assess whether and how this judgment was accurate, we need to consider the changing lifestyles of people in suburbs from the 1900s to the 1950s, identifying continuities as well as changes. In fairness, too, we must distinguish those elements of suburban life that were planned from those that developed unintentionally, in order to clarify what possibilities have been forgone.

Styles of Living, 1900–1960

In the early twentieth century there was no such thing as *the* suburban way of life. The available evidence on municipal services and the availability of home appliances hint at the diversity of suburban living. In the City of Hamilton in 1899 only four-fifths of dwellings had piped water; two-thirds had sewers. In recently annexed areas both proportions were far lower, barely 5 per cent. By 1921 piped services had become ubiquitous in the city, but a quarter of recently annexed territory – and surely a higher proportion of suburban homes – still lacked them. A national survey in about 1920 showed that in municipalities with a population of two thousand to twenty thousand, many of which would have been suburban, the incidence of piped sewerage ranged from 100 per cent to 20 per cent. For women, especially, these statistics indicate important differences in the conditions of suburban life. So, too, does the meagre evidence on home appliances. A survey of Ontario homes reported in *Electrical News* indicates that in 1925 only 16 per cent of Ontario households had washing machines, 14 per cent had electric stoves, and 19 per cent had vacuum cleaners. These percentages pertained to homes in all types of settlement, urban, suburban, and rural, but they speak to the varied conditions under which suburban residents lived and women worked.

The diversity of suburban ways of life was even greater than bare statistics can show. At one extreme were the lifestyles of the rich and powerful, almost all of whom, as David Ley has emphasized, were of British descent and drew upon British traditions to create socially exclusive patterns of behaviour. Homes and suburbs were social statements. Prestige was emphasized and tradition evoked by imitating Old World architecture: clients hired architects to design Scottish baronial castles, Gothic, Italianate, Second Empire, or Tudorbethan mansions. Size mattered. Women managed these homes with the help of an array of servants, including cooks, cleaners, and gardeners. They entertained other women of their class in 'at-home' tea parties, scheduled on fixed days of the week or month. Clear rules maintained subtle status distinctions. It was considered bad taste to visit a superior, though acceptable to leave a calling card and await an invitation. Garden parties were less exclusive, since they did not violate the privacy of the dwelling itself. Networks of visiting were complex. In Vancouver's West End, the *Elite Directory* of 1908 indicates the existence of five separate groups of at-home meetings on every day of the week. These defined separate geographical territories with little overlap, indicating how space was manipulated not only around but also within these elite suburbs.

Men attended garden parties, but not the at-homes, and took little interest in the running of the home. They spent their time at a club in town, where they added pleasure to business over lunch and a glass of port, or at golf, yacht, and country clubs, where business was added to pleasure. Women took themselves out of the home, too, usually by becoming involved in respectable voluntary work or amateur dramatics. Ley reports how, in the West End of Vancouver, a new arrival from England quickly joined the Ladies Aid, the Women's Auxiliary, the Women's Council of the YWCA, the Victorian Order of Nurses, the Anti-Tuberculosis Society, and the Ladies Minerva Club. These formal and semi-formal organizations solidified social networks, while private schools within or near the elite areas increased the likelihood that such networks would be perpetuated through social and academic training and, eventually, marriage into an appropriate family. In Vancouver's West End, Toronto's Forest Hill, and Montreal's West-mount, elite suburbs were distinct social worlds.

A long step down from the suburban lives of the social

elite was the more common experience of the middle class. In the late nineteenth and early twentieth centuries, servants became scarcer and less affordable. As women in middle-class households found it necessary to do their own housework, they learned to appreciate the virtues of a home that was easy to maintain. Simplicity and efficiency became the new watchwords. After the overstuffed Victorian era, furnishings became simpler. In 1904 a writer in *Canadian Magazine* deplored the 'lack of simplicity in our homes' and urged her women readers to moderate their desire to acquire ornaments that had to be dusted and elaborate furnishings that had to be cleaned. This moderation in furnishings was mandated by a new fashion to occupy smaller houses. Building permits indicate that, at the turn of the century in the City of Toronto, 64 per cent of all new houses had three storeys; by 1913 this proportion had fallen to 36 per cent. The same trend affected the suburbs.

To serve the needs of their occupants, smaller houses had to be designed more efficiently. Architects and builders began to pay much more attention to the functionality of interior space, especially the kitchen. Now that they had to do their own housework, women were attracted by the promise of new labour-saving technology. Electric irons were one of the first appliances to become popular and by 1925 were virtually ubiquitous in households with electricity. Vacuums and, in time, washing machines were also popular, but of all spaces in the middle-class home it was the kitchen that was most transformed. Kitchens became smaller and self-contained. Coal and wood stoves were large and required ancillary storage in the basement or backyard. Gas and electric stoves, which became common in the 1920s, were cleaner, convenient, and more compact. Refrigerators displaced ice boxes and encouraged a new rhythm of weekly shopping. As kitchens became cleaner and as servants became rare, the walls and doors that separated kitchens from living and dining rooms began to come down. It was only after 1945, however, that the open-plan kitchen, perhaps with an attached breakfast nook, became the norm.

The new emphasis upon efficiency accompanied a new type of pride in the home. Middle-class women had long prided themselves and had been judged on their ability to manage their households. In the early decades of the twentieth century middle-class men began to show a new interest. Margaret Marsh has detected the emergence of male domesticity at this time in the United States; this took the form of woodworking in the basement rather than of housework, and it extended to gardening. As well as being easier to keep clean, smaller houses were more affordable and, perhaps because the new male domesticity found expression in maintenance and repairs, it helped to make ownership more important. Working-class and immigrant families had long been willing to make great sacrifices in order to own their own houses, and by the 1920s ownership had also become a middle-class norm. This was the beginning of a class convergence in domestic and suburban values that eventually found expression in the mass suburb of the 1950s.

Life in the shacktown suburbs was different again. Here, men and women substituted their own labour for the services that the middle and upper classes were able to purchase. By 1910 senior executives might drive or be chauffeured to work, while accountants and teachers took the streetcar. Labourers, and even mechanics, were just as likely to walk as to take transit, even if doing so added a two-hour round trip to their working day. In the early years of settlement, men laboured in the evenings and on weekends to build and extend their houses, which often meant that they had no day of rest, since six-day work weeks were common. Unpaved roads resulted in dirty clothes, and without piped water women worked hard both to cook and to keep their families clean. To save money they often grew vegetables, made clothes, and raised chickens. Merchants made shopping easier by delivering coal, wood, meat, fish, bread and cakes, ice, tea, soft drinks, and household hardware, but to buy other goods women had to travel downtown, which entailed an expensive and time-consuming expedition. Daughters and occasionally sons, not servants, helped out. Vacuums, refrigerators, and washing machines were but distant rumours: advertising images in the newspaper or the Eaton's catalogue encouraged these suburban women to dream, but few had seen one of these appliances in action. Because of their long work days and long commutes, men were rarely at home; without the commute and with work days that were even longer, women were rarely anywhere else. In social terms, an exceptionally marked gender division of labour was the one thing that all suburbs had in common.

The social diversity of the suburbs was reflected in the landscape. Collectively, suburbs looked very different from one another. The stolid edifices of the affluent suburbs contrasted with the tidy two- or two-and-a-half-storey foursquares of the middling districts and with the functional frame shacks at the working-class and immigrant fringe. Even within many of these suburbs there was variety. The elite paid architects handsomely to design structures in well-known architectural idioms or a blend of familiar styles, but that were in their particularities unique. At the other extreme, although limited finances and imaginations did constrain what amateurs built, the staged process of construction and the irregular variation in street setbacks produced a varied scene. As Alice Randle observed of houses at Toronto's shacktown fringe in 1914, 'there are no two alike.' Only in the middle-class districts and on some of the speculatively built blocks in industrial suburbs was regularity a feature of the suburban landscape. In many suburbs, individuality had free play.

Early twentieth-century suburbs embodied the full diversity of Canadian society: immigrant and native-born, rich and poor. In that sense they were democratic in their opportunities. In addition, they made it possible for those at the bottom of the heap to improve their lot. Sweat equity and self-provisioning enabled families who could never have afforded to buy a house to make their own. Instead of cramming themselves into one or two rented rooms, these families used unregulated suburbs to realize better possibilities. In that sense, the geography of settlement did not simply mirror society but helped to constitute it.

Until the 1920s the priorities of workers and the middle classes differed. Professionals placed a high priority on the comfort and convenience of living near streetcar lines and of having basic municipal services. They would not live in unserviced suburbs, and as a result, such areas were avoided by builders who served the middle-class market. Home ownership was viewed as desirable, but less significant. In contrast, workers wanted security, something they could call their own, and would sacrifice anything to that end, whether it meant living without services and transit or taking in boarders.

The convergence of priorities that became apparent after 1918 occurred as middle-class families began to attach higher priority to home ownership, but adjustments also were made on the other side. Working families paid no heed to the middle-class reformers who advised them to stop taking in boarders; they continued to do so in large numbers until the 1950s. But as the incomes of a minority of the better-paid workers began to rise, cars, or at least appliances and packaged foods, became more readily available; and as the opportunities for owner-building came under pressure, especially in the larger urban centres, some suburban workers began to adopt a recognizably modern consumer lifestyle. Suzanne Morton sees this shift starting to happen in the Hydrostone district of Halifax during the 1920s, admittedly an untypical new development. It would be dangerous to overstate the point. Liz Cohen has pointed out that even the same brand product can be used differently by and have different meanings to different people. But in the 1920s segments of the working class did begin to move towards what we may now recognize as a more middle-class style of life. Significantly, perhaps, this was the last decade when front porches, for many years an important place for socialization in working-class neighbourhoods, were routinely included in the design of new houses.

The convergence in suburban living was halted, and even reversed, by the Great Depression. During the 1930s only quite affluent families in relatively secure jobs were in a position to acquire new houses; many suburban workers and their families reverted to self-provisioning and were content to get by. In 1937 the federal government launched the Home Improvement Plan, whose purpose, apart from creating jobs in the construction industry, was to modernize Canadian homes. It made provision for low-interest loans, many of which were targeted at updating kitchens. They were remodelled so that the large, inefficient room of the past, which had often served as a hub of household activities, became merely a place of work, tidier and more efficient but also isolated. Even more obviously, it encouraged a generic consumer lifestyle. About 10 per cent of Canadian households took advantage of this plan before it was cancelled in 1941. This number was substantial, but clearly, like the Dominion and National Housing acts, for the most part the Home Improvement Plan helped those who least needed it. It offered a model, but not an instrument, of assistance to working families. The convergence of suburban lifestyles that had begun during the 1920s did not resume until after 1945.

Although happening more slowly than many supposed, after 1945 the ways suburbanites chose or were compelled to live converged. Growing affluence made it possible for more suburban families to afford a car. In 1941, in the suburbs of major Canadian cities, fewer than half of all families owned a car. Indeed, the proportions varied greatly from place to place, extending from a low of 22 per cent in the suburbs of Quebec City to a high of 71 per cent in suburban Hamilton. By 1961 a large majority of families across the country had a car. By then, too, municipal services had become ubiquitous in the suburbs, as had appliances such as vacuums and refrigerators. In 1941 only 21 per cent of Canadian households had a mechanical refrigerator. During the late 1940s shipments soared, rising from a paltry 237 units in 1944 to a peak of 342,000 in 1950, before dropping back in the 1950s. By 1951 almost half of all households had a fridge and by 1961 the proportion exceeded 90 per cent. Washing machines had become very nearly as common, although a great majority still had separate wringers. Boarding and lodging, always less common in suburbs than in more central areas, dropped precipitously. After the austerity of the early post-war years, houses and lots soon expanded. As family life turned inwards towards the backyard and the rec room, porches lost their purpose.

The resurgence of owner-building in the late 1940s might seem to have delayed or even reversed this convergence in living styles, but in the end it became one of the routes to that end. By definition, owner-builders relied less on the market for the satisfaction of their needs, especially because some also saved money by growing fruit and vegetables. For a time, and in some areas, there were some striking juxtapositions. In Fleetwood, a district in Surrey, B.C., Leonard Evenden has described some poignant contrasts in the 1950s and 1960s. Older residents, some of whom had erected houses and helped to build a community centre, made productive but messy use of their properties, setting aside one corner for a garden, another for running car repairs, and yet another for handyman yardwork. Newer residents saw property as something to be bought, consumed, and sold: they favoured more reliable, late-model cars, and tidier, generic, low-maintenance yards, ready for quick sale. These were extremes, combining differences not only in age but also of class. In most areas, the contrasts were more subtle. After 1945 young owner-builders typically included men in a wide range of occupations. Buying conventional designs and materials, they produced houses and suburbs that were broadly similar to one another and differed little from those developed by the smaller professional builders. In the late 1950s, as the boom in owner-building evolved into home improvement, do-it-yourself became a characteristic element in the suburban way of life. Commercialized by the more progressive building supply dealers, it blended middle-class consumerism with the working-class tradition of home handiwork. Newer even than the amortized mortgage, it perfectly embodied the convergence in suburban styles of living. It became the way in which post-war suburbs incorporated individual expression.

Change and Continuity

In the six decades after 1900 suburbs had changed and in so doing had become more important. By 1960 they were more uniform and ubiquitous than ever and were leading symbols of a new consumer lifestyle. This way of life, which depended on the steady growth in real incomes after 1945, involved more than an increasing reliance on purchased goods and services. Credit was its hallmark; for credit made it possible for families to live beyond their immediate needs and means, to make materialism – of the sort that Seeley and his associates detected and deplored in post-war Crestwood Heights – a way of life. Credit fuelled the post-war economy, making it possible for people to acquire more and to live more comfortably and more privately. The amortizing mortgage was its foundation and the corporate suburb its first collective embodiment. Suburbs did not simply express debt-encumbered consumerism, they mandated it. As in the unplanned suburbs of the early twentieth century, suburban geography was crucial to a way of life. It is no wonder that so many contemporaries held it up as the symbol of the modern era.

The triumph of consumerism meant the defeat, largely unheralded, of thrift. Throughout the first half of the twentieth century thrift was an unquestioned virtue, a principle that guided the actions of households and governments alike. It meant conserving resources, paying one's way, and avoiding debt; in the case of unavoidable debts it meant retiring them as soon as possible. In ways that historians have not yet fully explored it was a great influence on federal policy, notably the Commission of Conservation (1909–21), which emphasized the conservation of all resources. For a time thrift continued to guide the actions of house buyers after 1945. Oral histories show that families put up with the hardships of building their own home in part to avoid debt. The experience of the Depression was still fresh in many minds. The attitude of thrift died hard, though its battles were not public. They were waged every time a household decided whether to build or to buy a house, to take on debt or to settle in far suburbs that required a car. Unencumbered by bitter memories, the generation that was eventually raised in the post-war suburbs embraced the new consumer lifestyle wholeheartedly.

The suburban changes were substantial, but there were also continuities. Throughout the twentieth century, suburbs have been defended and justified above all as the ideal places in which to bring up children. In 1909 a promotional booklet for the Parsons Estate, a Toronto subdivision that soon became an immigrant shacktown, extolled its virtues as an area where 'children, as well as grown people, thrive better on the air that sweeps fresh and free over the meadows and woods of the country.' The same spirit, combined with themes of nurturing and protection, has continued to inform real estate advertisements and in all segments of the market. Post-war suburbs were designed to suit the needs of young children. Culs-de-sac eliminated through traffic, and curves and T-junctions slowed it down. The result, supposedly, was safer streets. Apart from churches, schools were the only non-residential land use allowed throughout large parts of the suburbs, and in many subdivisions they were located so that children could readily reach them on foot.

Some of this planning was short-sighted and even misguided. Schools were spaced to serve communities in which most houses contained young families, which commonly comprised three or more children. Within less than a generation, some schools were redundant. More generally, environments that were arguably ideal for young children turned out to be less attractive to teenagers. The point is familiar to any suburban parent and was wryly underlined in a recent 'Bizarro' cartoon. Two couples are socializing around a backyard barbecue. 'We moved to the suburbs for the kids,' one of the women is saying, 'so they'll be bored out of their skulls and leave home as soon as they're 18.' The insight is not original. Families have rarely supposed that suburbs were in every way, and for all children, ideal. But for more than a century they have on balance viewed the suburbs as the best place to raise children, and land developers and builders have been very ready to accommodate those needs.

Because suburbs were built for children, they helped to define the place of women. One of the strongest continuities in the social character of suburbs between 1900 and the 1960s is the manner in which they embodied a sharp gender division of labour. Alice Randle caricatured the gentleman owner-builder in suburban Toronto in 1914: 'At night returning, every labor sped, / He sits him down the monarch of a shed.' Meanwhile, the neatness and cleanliness of the home, the curtained windows that show 'a thrifty woman's care,' and the 'sturdy children,' 'quite as immaculate ... as gleeful, lung-expanding outdoor games permit,' expressed the role of his consort. Some details are specific to the time and place. The man walks to work. The house, the curtains, and doubtless some of the clothes are home-made. But the sharp division of labour was familiar in the more affluent suburbs of the day and remained so for more than half a century. Pierre Vallières commented on his mother's prospective 'exile' from Montreal's East End with the family's move to suburban Longeuil in the late 1940s. Veronica Strong-Boag quotes a spokesman for a Toronto construction company in 1958; speaking about the suburban house, he observed: 'a man just boards there: he gets his meals,' while 'she is there all day long.' Similarly, Norman Pearson describes the post-war suburbs as a 'special compound' in which women were effectively 'locked away.' Betty Friedan also has explored the implications of this situation at great length and to great effect. For many decades, suburbs continued to isolate women.

In the early twentieth century, this isolation was relatively novel. Through an imaginative time-geographic reconstruction Roger Miller has suggested how, in the late nineteenth century, a move to the suburbs sharply reduced the ability of middle-class women to engage in urban activities. Such a move mattered more at this time than previously because servants were becoming scarcer and were especially reluctant to take positions in homes that were less accessible. Without servants, not only did women have to do more domestic work, but this work, notably cooking and childrearing, imposed narrow constraints on their free time. It was in this new context that a suburban location mattered. Of course, the lives of women in working families had always been governed by such constraints. The novelty was that it was only in the early twentieth century that significant numbers of working families were able to move into fairly distant suburbs. They might previously have settled at the urban fringe, perhaps in an industrial suburb, but they were still likely to be within walking distance of retail strips and centres. After 1900 the streetcar suburbs and the suburbs that grew up beyond the end of the lines imposed a new isolation. In various forms it was an isolation that persisted well into the post-war period until large numbers of women entered the labour force and acquired automobiles. Of course, for some time women's geographical isolation made it difficult for them to enter the labour force. That is one of the reasons, as Pierre Drouilly has shown for Montreal, that labour force participation rates for women in the early post-war years were so much higher in centrally located urban neighbourhoods than in the outer reaches of the urban area. Feminists have made much of Virginia Woolf's call for a Room of One's Own. Arguably, however, of the available cures for the suburban problem that had no name the most important one turned out to be the acquisition of a car of one's own. This only began to happen in large numbers in the 1960s and 1970s. In terms of the way they isolated women, then, the suburbs of the 1950s had more in common with those of the 1900s than those of today. They expressed an important continuity, on the cusp of change.

Intentions and Effects

It is difficult not to see the evolution of Canadian suburbs as the inevitable expression of historical forces, including the intentions of those who settled in them. People needed homes and wanted space; new transportation technologies brought cheaper suburban land within the reach of many; rising incomes made it feasible for governments to mandate (and enforce) building standards for health and safety. Land subdividers, developers, builders, and lenders were happy to oblige. What else is there to say? It is true that these trends were bound to shape the suburbs. It is also true that suburbs were, and still are, artificial constructions. Created through the deliberate actions of many people, they are in that sense planned. But the effects of our actions routinely differ from our intentions. In constructing this history of Canadian suburbs between 1900 and 1960, I have tried to identify several periods, or moments, when actions did not have the desired effects, when things might have been done differently and better.

One of the more obvious examples of unintended misfortune was the unplanned suburbs of the early decades of the twentieth century. Settlers hoped to build for themselves affordable and healthy houses in which to raise children. The nature and scattering of initial settlement caused problems. People relied on wells and privies; when blocks filled up, their health was threatened. Services had to be installed, and because they followed the house-building phase, they cost far more than necessary. Taxes rose, families got into financial trouble, fell into arrears, and so created difficulties for suburban governments. In retrospect, this was a predictable chain of events. A little planning might have gone a long way: subdivision controls might have prevented scattered development; installed earlier, basic services would have raised the initial cost of land and perhaps excluded a few of the very poorest of families, but in the long run they would have kept taxes down and saved many from ruin. Unfortunately, no one had the foresight and ability to forestall what turned into a tragedy for thousands, and in any event the political will was lacking.

Another series of actions with unintended consequences were the progressive elaboration of building regulations and subdivision controls. In an urbanized area some restraints over construction are clearly necessary. Such controls were advocated and extended throughout the twentieth century. In some instances they were used by local municipalities in order to prevent undesirable sorts of development. In general, however, those who promoted controls did so with good intentions and apparently with little appreciation for their exclusionary effects. As various national guidelines were formulated, mandated for NHA construction, and widely adopted after 1945, they defined the suburbs as off limits to those with low and moderate incomes. Compromises might have allowed lower-income families to build in stages; to occupy unfinished dwellings; to manage in small houses on small lots with minimal services. The resulting suburbs might not have looked impressive, but they could have been perfectly safe and healthy. Instead, the post-war growth of corporate suburbs has reduced suburban diversity and confined lower-income families to the central city.

The list of unintended consequences could be extended further. From the 1900s to the 1960s few probably fully appreciated the degree of isolation that many women would experience as they moved to the suburbs. Each suburban generation had to learn this lesson anew. The same is true of the steady growth in home ownership that suburbanization has made possible. The majority of Canadian families and the overwhelming majority of social commentators have viewed home ownership as an unmitigated blessing, but it has its downside. Homeowners care more about their neighbourhood and strongly resist the incursion of land uses and individuals that they consider to be undesirable. The processes of exclusion that are so powerful in the United States have also played a role in Canadian suburbs. In effect, though rarely by design, they have been strengthened by the norm of owner-occupation.

Not all unintended consequences have been negative. In the early years of the century several streetcar companies were reluctant to extend their lines beyond, or even as far as, the suburban built-up fringe. They acted from self-interest, knowing that suburban lines were the least profitable, and they were heedless of the complaints of suburban riders. The effect, most obviously in Toronto, was to force land subdividers to create small-lot suburbs. In time, as they developed high densities, these suburbs encouraged the extension of transit, in the form of either fixed rail systems or bus lines. Today, these are the sorts of urban density that advocates of the New Urbanism endorse.

In general, however, hindsight indicates that matters could have been handled more effectively. In the early twentieth century the suburbs needed more regulation; by the late 1950s they needed less. In all periods they might have been encouraged to accommodate tenants. In the post-war years governments should have restrained the capitulation of suburbs to the automobile. In addition to moderating these trends that were already under way, what could Canadians, and more specifically our governments, have done to make suburbs better? Historical observers have suggested that two actions, in particular, could usefully have been taken.

During the 1910s, when the automobile was beginning to be seen as a serious form of urban transportation, there was a short-lived boom in jitneys. For a time they were a popular alternative to crowded and inflexible streetcars. At the behest of the transit companies, local governments soon imposed controls on the jitney operators and in the 1920s regulated them out of existence. Donald Davis has argued that, if governments instead had nurtured and channelled the nascent jitney industry, they might have fashioned an alternative, flexible form of suburban transportation. Commuters then would not have been forced to choose between the streetcar and the automobile, an unequal contest that eventually produced auto-oriented sprawl.

House building was a second field of action in which governments might have encouraged suburbs to develop differently. Throughout the first half of the twentieth century, hundreds of thousands of Canadians built their own suburban houses. In the great majority of cases they received no assistance from the state; more commonly, they were discouraged and disparaged. As the 'small homes' program of the City of Stockholm had shown after 1927 and as a program under the Veterans' Land Act was to prove after 1948, the energy and commitment of amateurs could easily be guided to create attractive and inexpensive suburban homes. Instead, however, from the mid-1930s onward federal housing programs were single-mindedly directed at fostering the growth of institutional mortgage finance and, after 1945, of the corporate suburb. The resulting uniformity was what exercised contemporary critics, but the more serious consequence was surely the exclusion of a significant minority of Canadian families. For these reasons, the post-war Canadian suburb could have been more socially inclusive and less reliant upon the privately owned car than it turned out to be. Many judged it to be good, and after years of austerity and war it almost seemed like the promised land, but it could have been better.

Creeping Conformity

In Britain, some writers had begun to speak of suburban conformity in the early nineteenth century, and by 1900, especially in London, this feature was being lampooned. In Canada the same criticism did not emerge until after 1945, when the corporate suburb became dominant. How accurate, and how important, is the charge?

In one sense, the growing conformity of the post-war suburbs did not run as deep as many observers supposed. A three-bedroom house, a mortgage, a car, and three children did not make everyone the same. Even in as regulated a suburb as Thorncrest Village there was the cultural space to express a wide range of hobbies, tastes, and interests, as well as political and religious views. Outsiders, styling themselves as urban sophisticates, liked to sneer. But as often as not they were selecting and responding to stereotypes of their own invention, rather than to the diversity that survived and thrived, albeit most commonly in the privacy of people's homes.

Some of the uniformity of the early post-war suburbs was temporary. For an exceptional combination of reasons, there was an unprecedented number of new couples who were buying houses and having children at about the same time. The families that made up this generation aged together, of course, but as they became more mobile, the demography of the suburbs that they had first occupied became more varied. The age composition and family structure of suburbs had never been so simplified, so easy to stereotype, as they were in the 1950s, and they may never be again.

In one important respect the conformity of the corporate suburbs has steadily become more profound. The mass consumption of the 1950s, in which it seemed that everyone watched *I Love Lucy* and bought either a Chevrolet or a Ford, might seem very different from the multi-channel cornucopia that confronts the modern suburbanite. It is possible to identify an early post-war suburb at a glance: modest single-detached houses, minimal eaves (because of a shortage of materials), picture windows, 'teardrop' doors, and in the middle-class areas a comfortable ranch-style sprawl. The same is not true today. Subdivisions contain a mix of detached and semi-detached houses, row housing, and sometimes medium- and high-rise condominiums. These buildings come in a variety of retro styles, ranging from neo-Gothic, through California bungalow, to postmodern pastiche, all combined and modulated to accommodate regional tastes and traditions. Where once there was conformity, there might now seem to be choice, and then some. But the deeper conformity of the post-war suburbs was the way that they mandated a high level of consumption, encouraging people to define themselves through what they purchased by acquiring debt. Swapping tail fins for 4WD, we have travelled further down that suburban road, and as yet there is no end in sight. When we round the next curve, however, we may discover that, ignoring the sign at the last turn, we are heading up a cul-de-sac with no turning space at the end.

To stretch the argument, but not beyond the breaking point, we might say that the lifestyle first perfected in the early post-war suburbs has returned to conquer the city. Chains such as Tim Hortons and Indigo, which were weaned and grew strong in the suburbs, have returned to conquer the city. Sometimes they have aroused opposition from those who value the authenticity of the neighbourhood café, the autonomy of the small bookstore. But even this opposition can seem tainted. No less, and in some ways more obviously than the doughnut shop and chain bookstore, authenticated neighbourhoods, heritage districts, and revived farmers' markets encourage us to define our-

selves through what and how we buy. This is a simple extension of how post-war developers sold their packaged
subdivisions. Beneath the surface kaleidoscope, the conformity that was pioneered in the corporate suburbs is
carrying the day.

Bibliography

Bibliographic Essay

For a general discussion of the suburban way of life, with an emphasis on North America in the post-war period, see Herbert Gans, 'Urbanism and Suburbanism as Ways of Life: A Re-evaluation of Definitions,' in Herbert J. Gans, *People and Plans: Essays on Urban Problems and Solutions* (New York: Basic Books, 1968); Scott Donaldson, *The Suburban Myth* (New York: Columbia University Press, 1968). For an influential survey of modern urban and suburban landscapes, with Canadian examples, see Edward Relph, *The Modern Urban Landscape* (Baltimore, Md.: Johns Hopkins University Press, 1987). Planning influences are discussed in John Sewell. *The Shape of the City: Toronto Struggles with Modern Planning* (Toronto: University of Toronto Press, 1993); Gerald Hodge, *Planning Canadian Communities: An Introduction to the Principles, Practice and Participants* (Scarborough, Ont.: Nelson Canada, 1991). Processes of land development and construction are treated at length in Michael Doucet and John Weaver, *Housing the North American City* (Montreal and Kingston: McGill-Queen's University Press, 1991). Early forms of Canadian housing are discussed and illustrated by Peter Ennals and Deryck Holdsworth in *Homeplace: The Making of the Canadian Dwelling over Three Centuries* (Toronto: University of Toronto Press, 1998), while many aspects of post-war housing are surveyed in a collection edited by John Miron, *House, Home and Community: Progress in Housing Canadians, 1945–1986* (Montreal and Kingston: McGill-Queen's University Press, 1993). For a survey and reinterpretation of the literature on North American cities and suburbs see Richard Harris and Robert Lewis, 'The Geography of North American Cities and Suburbs, 1900–1950: A New Synthesis,' *Journal of Urban History* 27,3 (2001): 262–93. For perspectives on Canadian-U.S. urban differences see Richard Harris, 'Canadian Cities in a North American Context,' in *North America: The Historical Geography of a Changing Continent*, ed. Thomas McIlwraith and Ted Muller, 2nd ed. (Boulder, Co.: Rowman and Littlefield, 2001).

There is no survey of Canadian suburbs in the twentieth century, but on western cities see L.D. McCann, *John Olmsted's Masterpiece: The Uplands and Suburban Development in Western Canada* (forthcoming). For early decades see L.D. McCann, 'Suburbs of Desire: The Suburban Landscape of Canadian Cities, c.1900–1950,' in *Changing Suburbs: Foundation, Form and Function*, ed. Richard Harris and Peter Larkham (London: E and FN Spon, 1999). On post-war suburbs see Leonard J. Evenden and Gerald E. Walker, 'From Periphery to Centre: The Changing Geography of the Suburbs,' in *The Changing Social Geography of Canadian Cities*, ed. Larry S. Bourne and David F. Ley (Montreal and Kingston: McGill-Queen's University Press, 1993), and Veronica Strong-Boag, 'Home Dreams: Women and the Suburban Experiment in Canada, 1945–60,' *Canadian Historical Review* 72,4 (1991): 471–504.

The most systematic sequence of studies of suburbs in any urban area are of Toronto. See Peter G. Goheen, 'Victorian Toronto, 1950–1900: Pattern and Process of Growth,' University of Chicago, Department of Geography Research Paper No. 127; Richard Harris, *Unplanned Suburbs: Toronto's American Tragedy, 1900–1950* (Baltimore, Md.: Johns Hopkins University Press, 1996); Robert A Murdie, 'Factorial Ecology of Metropolitan Toronto, 1951–1961,' University of Chicago, Department of Geography Research Paper No. 116; Samuel D. Clark, *The Suburban Society* (Toronto: University of Toronto Press, 1966). On Montreal see Walter van Nus, 'A Community of Communities:

Suburbs in the Development of "Greater Montreal,'" in *Montreal Metropolis, 1886–1930*, ed. Isabelle Gournay and France Vanlaethem (Montreal: Canadian Centre for Architecture, 1998); on Vancouver see Graeme Wynn, 'The Rise of Vancouver,' in *Vancouver and Its Region*, ed. Graeme Wynn and Timothy Oke (Vancouver: UBC Press, 1992). The most complete history of any suburb is Bruce Elliott, *The City Beyond: A History of Nepean, Birthplace of Canada's Capital, 1792–1990* (Nepean: City of Nepean, 1991). For case studies of specific types of suburbs see, especially, John Weaver's study of a middle-class suburb, 'From Land Assembly to Social Maturity: The Suburban Life of Westdale (Hamilton), Ontario, 1911–1951,' *Histoire sociale / Social History* 11 (1978): 411–40; the detailed examination of an industrial suburb by Paul-André Linteau, *The Promoters' City: Building the Industrial Town of Maisonneuve, 1883–1918* (Toronto: Lorimer, 1985); Richard Harris's study of unplanned suburbs (above); and on an affluent suburb see John R. Seeley, R.A. Sim, and E.W. Loosley, *Crestwood Heights: A Study of the Culture of Suburban Life* (Toronto: University of Toronto Press, 1956). The last, together with Etan Diamond, *And I Will Dwell in their Midst: Orthodox Jews in Suburbia* (Chapel Hill.: University of North Carolina Press, 2000), constitutes the fullest account of the early suburban migration of an ethnic minority. An exceptional study of the industrial aspects of suburban development is Robert Lewis, *Manufacturing Montreal: The Making of an Industrial Landscape* (Baltimore, Md.: Johns Hopkins University Press, 2000).

Evocative oral histories, describing life in unplanned suburbs, are collected in Bill Bailey, *Stories of York* (Toronto: Bill Bailey, 1981). For references on specific places see Alan F.J.Artibise and Gilbert Stelter, *Canada's Urban Past: Bibliography to 1980 and Guide to Canadian Urban Studies* (Vancouver: UBC Press, 1981). For a while this document was updated annually in the Canadian publication, *Urban History Review*. This journal is the main location of published studies of Canadian suburbs. Its historical table of contents is posted on its Web site, http://www.fas.umontreal.ca/HST/urbanhistory/contentsenglish.html. For debates about the history of cities and suburbs in Canada and the United States, see the daily log for 'H-Urban,' the discussion list for urban historians, at http://www2.h-net.msu.edu/~urban/. The home page for 'H-Urban' includes an extensive webography and links, some of which deal specifically with suburbs. The fall 2001 issue of *Urban History Review* contains a critical review of urban historical websites.

∾

The authors of many of the references cited in this essay are mentioned by name in the text, and are *not* usually cited under specific chapters. In the following bibliography, publications are usually cited only once, when they are first relevant.

Chapter 1 Introduction

Baxandall, Rosalyn, and Elizabeth Ewen. *Picture Windows: How the Suburbs Happened*. New York: Basic Books, 2000.

Carver, Humphrey. 'Building the Suburbs: A Planner's Reflections.' *City Magazine* 3,7 (1978): 40–5.

Clark, S.D. *The Suburban Society*. Toronto: University of Toronto Press, 1966.

Dale, Stephen. *Lost in the Suburbs*. Toronto: Stoddart, 1999.

Garner, Hugh. 'You Take the Suburbs ... I Don't Want Them.' *Maclean's* (10 Nov. 1954): 71–5.

Gray, John. 'Why Live in the Suburbs?' *Maclean's* (1 Sept. 1954): 7–11, 50–2.

Hanna, David B. 'Creation of an Early Victorian Suburb.' *Urban History Review* 9,2 (1980): 38–64.

Iacovetta, Franca. 'Gossip, Contest, and Power in the Making of Suburban Bad Girls: Toronto, 1945–60.' *Canadian Historical Review* 80,4 (1999): 585–623.

Korinek, Valerie. *Roughing It in the Suburbs. Reading Chatelaine Magazine in the Fifties and Sixties*. Toronto: University of Toronto Press, 2000.

Lorimer, Peter. *The Developers*. Toronto: Lorimer, 1976.

Moore, Peter. 'Public Services and Residential Development in a Toronto Neighborhood, 1880–1915.' *Journal of Urban History* 9,4 (1983): 445–71.

Morton, Suzanne. *Ideal Surroundings: Domestic Life in a Working-Class Suburb in the 1920s.* Toronto: University of Toronto Press, 1995.

Reissman, David. *The Lonely Crowd: A Study of the Changing American Character.* New Haven, Conn.: Yale University Press, 1950.

Thompson, F.M.L. 'Introduction: The Rise of Suburbia.' In *The Rise of Suburbia*, ed. F.M.L.Thompson, 2–24. Leicester: Leicester University Press, 1982.

Vallières, Pierre. *White Niggers of America.* Toronto: McClelland and Stewart, 1971.

Weiss, Marc. *The Rise of the Community Builders: The American Real Estate Industry and Urban Land Planning.* New York: Columbia University Press, 1987.

Whyte, William H. *The Organization Man.* New York: Doubleday, 1956.

Chapter 2 A Place and a People

Baillargeon, Denyse. *Making Do: Women, Family and Home in Montreal during the Great Depression.* Waterloo, Ont.: Wilfrid Laurier University Press, 1999.

Bridle, Augustus. 'The Homes of Workingmen.' *Canadian Magazine* 22,1 (1903/4): 33–40.

Bryson, Lois, and Ian Winter. *Social Change, Suburban Lives: An Australian Newtown, 1960s to 1990s.* Sydney: Allen and Unwin, 1999.

Choko, Marc. *Une Cité-Jardin à Montréal : La Cité-Jardin du Tricentenaire, 1940–1947.* Montreal: Méridien, 1989.

– Ethnicity and Home Ownership in Montreal, 1921–51. *Urban History Review* 26,2 (1998): 36–41.

Collin, J.-P. 'A Housing Model for Lower and Middle-Class Wage Earners in a Montreal Suburb: Saint-Léonard, 1955–1967.' *Journal of Urban History* 24,4 (1998): 468–90.

Copp, Terry. *The Anatomy of Poverty: The Condition of the Working Class in Montreal, 1897–1929*. Toronto: McClelland and Stewart, 1974.

Cox, Kevin R. 'Housing Tenure and Neighborhood Activism.' *Urban Affairs Quarterly* 18,1 (1982): 107–29.

Dennis, Richard. 'Apartment Housing in Canadian Cities, 1900–1940.' *Urban History Review* 26,2 (1998): 17–31.

Doucet, Michael, and John Weaver. *Housing the North American City*. Montreal and Kingston: McGill-Queen's University Press, 1991.

Drouilly, Pierre. *L'espace social de Montréal, 1951–1991*. Sillery: Septentrion, 1996.

Edel, Matthew, Elliott D.Sclar, and Daniel Luria. *Shaky Palaces: Homeownership and Social Mobility in Boston's Suburbanization*. New York: Columbia University Press, 1984.

Fishman, Robert. *Bourgeois Utopias: The Rise and Fall of Suburbia*. New York: Basic Books, 1987.

Friedan, Betty. *The Feminine Mystique*. New York: Norton, 1963.

Hagopian, John. 'Galt's "Dickson's Hill": The Evolution of a Late-Victorian Neighbourhood in an Ontario Town.' *Urban History Review* 27,2 (1999): 25–43.

Harris, Richard. *Unplanned Suburbs: Toronto's American Tragedy, 1900–1950*. Baltimore, Md.: Johns Hopkins University Press, 1996.

Harris, Richard, and Chris Hamnett. 'The Myth of the Promised Land: The Social Diffusion of Home Ownership in Britain and North America.' *Annals of the Association of American Geographers* 77,2 (1987): 173–90.

Harris, Richard, and Peter Larkham. *Changing Suburbs: Foundation, Form and Function*. London: E and FN Spon, 1999.

Hayden, Dolores. *Building Suburbia: Green Fields and Urban Growth, 1820–2000*. New York: Pantheon, 2003

Henderson, Harry. 'The Mass-Produced Suburbs.' *Harper's* 207 (Nov. 1953): 25–32; 207 (Dec. 1953): 80–6.

Jackson, Kenneth T. *Crabgrass Frontier: The Suburbanization of the United States*. New York: Oxford University Press, 1985.

Marsh, Margaret. 'Suburban Men and Masculine Domesticity, 1870–1915.' *American Quarterly* 40,4 (1988): 165–86.

Maclean-Hunter Publishing Company. *The Housing Plans of Canadians.* Toronto: Maclean-Hunter, 1945.

McCall, Frances V. *Vignettes of Early Winnipeg, 1912–1926.* Winnipeg: Frances V. McCall, 1981.

Mercier, Michael, and Christopher Boone. 'Infant Mortality in Ottawa, Canada, 1901: Assessing Cultural, Economic and Environmental Factors.' *Journal of Historical Geography* 28,4 (2002): 486–507.

Michelson, William H. *Man and His Urban Environment: A Sociological Approach.* Don Mills, Ont.: Addison-Wesley, 1976.

– *Environmental Choice, Human Behavior and Residential Satisfaction.* New York: Oxford University Press, 1977.

Moore, Peter W. 'Zoning and Planning: The Toronto Experience, 1904–1970.' In *The Usable Urban Past,* ed. A.F.J. Artibise and G. Stelter, 316–41. Toronto: Macmillan, 1979.

Pearson, Norman. 'Hell Is a Suburb.' *Community Planning Review* 7,3 (1957): 124–28.

Pratt, Geraldine. 'Housing Tenure and Social Cleavages in Urban Canada.' *Annals of the Association of American Geographers* 76 (1986): 366–80.

Randle, Alice. 'Suburban Settlement.' *Saturday Night* (3 Jan. 1914): 9.

Schulz, Patricia. *The East York Workers' Association: A Response to the Great Depression.* Toronto: New Hogtown Press, 1975

Sheils, Jean E., and Ben Swankey. *Work and Wages.* Vancouver: Trade Union Research Bureau, 1977.

Steeves, Dorothy G. *The Compassionate Rebel.* Vancouver: J.J. Douglas, 1977.

Strong-Boag, Veronica. 'Home Dreams: Women and the Suburban Experiment in Canada, 1945–60.' *Canadian Historical Review* 72,4 (1991): 471–504.

Tallman, Irving, and Ramona Morgner. 'Life-Style Differences among Urban and Suburban Blue Collar Families.' *Social Forces* 48 (1970): 334–48.

Thornton, Patricia, and Sherry Olson. 'A Deadly Discrimination
among Montreal Infants 1860–1900.' *Continuity and Change*
16,1 (2001): 95–135
Troy, Pat. 'Suburbs of Acquiescence, Suburbs of Protest.' *Housing Studies* 15,5 (2000): 717–38.
Weaver, John C. 'The Property Industry and Land Use Controls:
The Vancouver Experience, 1910–1945.' *Plan Canada* 19, 3–4
(1979): 211–25.
– 'From Land Assembly to Social Maturity: The Suburban Life of
Westdale (Hamilton), Ontario, 1911–1951.' *Histoire sociale /
Social History* 21 (1988): 411–40.
Wilmott, Peter, and Michael Young. *Family and Class in a London Suburb.* London: Routledge and Kegan Paul, 1960.

Chapter 3 Cities and Suburbs

Ames, Herbert. *The City below the Hill.* Montreal: Bishop Engraving.
Baskerville, Peter. 'Home Ownership and Spacious Homes:
Equity under Stress in Early Twentieth-Century Canada.' *Journal of Family History* 26,2 (2001): 272–88.
– 'Familiar Strangers: Urban Families with Boarders, Canada,
1901,' *Social Science History* 25,3 (1991): 321–46.
Bloomfield, Elizabeth, Gerald Bloomfield, and Marc Vallières.
'Urban Industrial Development in Central Canada.' In *Historical Atlas of Canada.* Vol. 3. *Addressing the Twentieth Century,
1891–1961,* ed. Donald Kerr and Deryck Holdsworth, plate 13.
Toronto: University of Toronto Press, 1990.
Bureau of Municipal Research. *What Is the Ward Going to Do with Toronto?* Toronto: Bureau of Municipal Research, 1917.
Burgess, Ernest W. 'The Growth of the City.' In *The City,* ed.
Robert E. Park, Ernest W. Burgess, and Roderick D. McKenzie,
47–62. Chicago: University of Chicago Press.
Davis, Donald. 'North American Urban Mass Transit, 1890–1950:
What If We Thought about It as a Type of Technology?' *History and Technology* 12 (1995): 309–25.
Douglass, Harlan. *The Suburban Trend.* New York: Century, 1925.

Ferguson, G.H. 'Decentralization of Industry and Metropolitan Control.' *Journal of the Town Planning Institute of Canada* 2,2 (1923): 13–14; 2,3 (1923): 5–12.

Foran, Max. 'Land Development Patterns in Calgary, 1884–1945.' In *The Usable Urban Past*, ed. Alan F.J. Artibise and Gilbert A. Stelter, 293–315. Toronto: Macmillan, 1979.

Gilliland, Jason, and Sherry Olson. 'Claims on Housing Space in Nineteenth-Century Montreal.' *Urban History Review* 26,2 (1998): 3–16.

Hall, Peter. *Cities of Tomorrow: An Intellectual History of Urban Planning and Design in the Twentieth Century.* Cambridge, Mass.: Blackwell, 1996.

Harney, Robert. *Gathering Place: Peoples and Neighbourhoods of Toronto, 1834–1945.* Toronto: University of Toronto Press, 1985.

Harris, Richard. 'The End Justified the Means: Boarding and Rooming in a City of Homes, 1891–1951.' *Journal of Social History* 26,2 (1992): 331–58.

Harris, Richard, and A. Victoria Bloomfield. 'The Impact of Industrial Decentralization on the Gendered Journey to Work, 1900–1940.' *Economic Geography* 73 (1997): 94–117.

Howard, Ebenezer. *Garden Cities of Tomorrow.* London: Faber and Faber, 1946 [orig. pub. 1898].

Hurl, Lorna. 'The Toronto Housing Company, 1912–1923: The Pitfalls of Painless Philanthropy.' *Canadian Historical Review* 65,1 (1984): 28–53.

Lewis, Robert. 'Running Rings around the City: North American Industrial Suburbs, 1850–1950.' In *Changing Suburbs: Foundation, Form and Function*, ed. Richard Harris and Peter Larkham, 146–67. London: E and FN Spon, 1999.

Mayne, Alan. *The Imagined Slum: Newspaper Representation in Three Cities, 1870–1914.* Leicester, U.K.: Leicester University Press, 1993.

Modell, John, and Hareven, Tamara. 'Urbanization and the Malleable Household.' *Journal of Marriage and the Family* 35 (1973): 467–79.

Piva, Michael. *The Condition of the Working Class in Toronto, 1900–1921.* Ottawa: University of Ottawa Press, 1979.

Purdy, Sean. '"This Is Not a Company; It Is a Cause": Class, Gender and the Toronto Housing Company, 1912–1920.' *Urban History Review* 21,2 (1993): 75–91.

Roberts, Gerrylynn K. 'Transport in the Twentieth Century City – Automobility.' In *American Cities and Technology*, ed. Gerrylynn K. Roberts and Philip Stedman, 53–92. New York: Routledge, 1999.

Rutherford, Paul. 'Tomorrow's Metropolis: The Urban Reform Movement in Canada, 1880–1920.' In *The Canadian City: Essays in Urban History*, ed. Gilbert A. Stelter and Alan F.J. Artibise, 368–92. Toronto: McClelland and Stewart, 1977.

Smith, Peter J. 'Land Development in Edmonton.' In *Historical Atlas of Canada*. Vol. 3. *Addressing the Twentieth Century, 1891–1961*, ed. Donald Kerr and Deryck Holdsworth, Plate 20. Toronto: University of Toronto Press, 1990.

Stone, Leroy O. *Urban Development in Canada*. Ottawa: Dominion Bureau of Statistics, 1967.

Warner, Sam Bass. *Streetcar Suburbs: The Process of Growth in Boston, 1870–1900*. Cambridge, Mass.: Harvard University Press, 1962.

Weaver, John C. '"Tomorrow's Metropolis Revisited: A Critical Assessment of Urban Reform in Canada, 1890–1920.' In *The Canadian City: Essays in Urban History*, ed. Gilbert A. Stelter and Alan F.J. Artibise, 393–418. Toronto: McClelland and Stewart, 1977.

Wirth, Louis. 'Urbanism as a Way of Life.' In *Classic Essays on the Culture of Cities*, ed. Richard Sennett, 143–64. New York: Appleton-Century-Crofts, 1969 [orig. pub. 1938].

Woodsworth, James S. *My Neighbor*. Toronto: University of Toronto Press, 1972 [orig. pub. 1911].

Chapter 4 The Making of Suburban Diversity, 1900–1929

Adams, Thomas. 'Bad Housing Conditions.' *Town Planning and Conservation of Life* 7,1 (1921): 12–15.

Anderson, Kay. *Vancouver's Chinatown: Racial Discourse in Canada, 1875–1980*. Montreal and Kingston: McGill-Queen's University Press, 1991.

Artibise, Alan F.J. *Winnipeg: A Social History of Urban Growth, 1874–1914.* Montreal and Kingston: McGill-Queen's University Press, 1975.

Clairmont, Donald H., and Dennis W. Magill. *Africville: The Life and Death of a Canadian Black Community.* Toronto: Canadian Scholar's Press, 1987.

Copping, Alfred E. *The Golden Land: The True Story and Experiences of Settlers in Canada.* London: Hodder and Stoughton, 1912.

Crone, Kennedy. 'Housing in Montreal.' *Social Welfare* (Nov. 1920): 41.

Dalzell, Arthur G. 'Should Shack-Towns Be Encouraged? *Canadian Engineer* 50 (23 March 1926): 411–15, and *Town Planning* 5,2 (April 1926): 23–9,

– *Housing in Canada.* Vol. 1. *Housing in Relation to Land Development.* Toronto: Social Service Council of Canada, 1927.

– *Housing in Canada.* Vol. 2. *The Housing of the Working Classes.* Toronto: Social Service Council of Canada, 1928.

Darroch, Gordon. 'Urban Ethnicity in Canada: Personal Assimilation and Political Communities.' *Canadian Review of Sociology and Anthropology* 18,1 (1981): 93–100.

Davey, Ian, and Michael Doucet. 'The Social Geography of a Commercial City.' In *The People of Hamilton, Canada West,* ed. Michael Katz, 319–42. Cambridge, Mass.: Harvard University Press, 1975.

Driedger, Leo, and G. Church. 'Residential Segregation and Institutional Completeness: A Comparison of Ethnic Minorities.' *Canadian Review of Sociology and Anthropology* 11,1 (1974): 30–52.

Duncan, Otis D., and Beverly Duncan. 'Occupational Stratification and Residential Distribution.' *American Journal of Sociology* 64 (1955): 364–74.

Dyos, Harold J., and David A. Reeder. 'Slums and Suburbs.' In *The Victorian City: Images and Realities.* Vol. 2. *Shapes on the Ground and A Change of Accent,* ed. Harold J. Dyos and Michael Wolff, 359–86. London: Routledge and Kegan Paul, 1973.

Engels, Friedrich. *The Condition of the Working Class in England.* London: Panther, 1969 (orig. pub. 1844).

Forward, Charles N. 'The Immortality of a Fashionable Residential District: The Uplands.' In *Residential and Neighbourhood Studies in Victoria*, ed. Charles N. Forward, 1–39. Victoria, B.C.: University of Victoria, 1973.

Fripp, R.M. 'Speculations on the Problem of Housing the Working Classes in Vancouver.' *Engineering and Contract Record* 28,41 (1914): 1276–8.

Gilpin, John F. 'Urban Land Speculation in the Development of Strathcona (South Edmonton) 1891–1912.' In *The Developing West: Essays in Canadian History in Honour of Lewis H. Thomas*, ed. John E. Foster, 179–199. Edmonton: University of Alberta Press, 1983.

Gowans, Alan. *The Comfortable House: North American Suburban Architecture, 1890–1930*. Cambridge, Mass.: MIT Press, 1986.

Harris, Richard. 'Residential Segregation and Class Formation in Canadian Cities: A Critical Review.' *Canadian Geographer* 28,2 (1984): 186–96.

Harris, Richard, and Doris Ragonetti. 'Where Credit Is Due: Residential Mortgage Finance in Canada, 1900–1954.' *Journal of Real Estate Finance and Economics* 16,2 (1998): 223–38.

Hiebert, Daniel. 'Class, Ethnicity and Residential Structure: The Social Geography of Winnipeg, 1901–21.' *Journal of Historical Geography* 17,1 (1991): 56–86.

– 'The Social Geography of Toronto in 1931: A Study of Residential Differentiation and Social Structure.' *Journal of Historical Geography* 21,1 (1995): 55–74.

Holdsworth, Deryck W. 'House and Home in Vancouver. Images of West Coast Urbanism.' *The Canadian City: Essays in Urban History*, ed. Gilbert A. Stelter and Alan F.J. Artibise, 186–211. Toronto: McClelland and Stewart, 1977.

Lewis, Robert. 'Class Residential Patterns and the Development of Industrial Districts in Montreal, 1861 and 1901.' *Journal of Urban History* 17,2 (1991): 123–52.

Mills, G.E. *Buying Wood and Building Farms: Marketing Lumber and Farm Building Designs on the Canadian Prairies, 1880 to 1920*. Ottawa: Parks Service, 1991.

Modell, John. 'Suburbanization and Change in the American
Family.' *Journal of Interdisciplinary History* 9 (1979): 621–46.
Paterson, Ross. 'Housing Finance in Early 20th Century Subur-
ban Toronto.' *Urban History Review* 20,2 (1991): 63–71.
Smith, Peter J. 'Land Development in Edmonton.' In *Historical
Atlas of Canada*. Vol. 3. *Addressing the Twentieth Century, 1891–
1961*, ed. Donald Kerr and Deryck Holdsworth, Plate 20.
Toronto: University of Toronto Press, 1990.
Stevenson, Katherine C., and H. Ward Jandl. *Houses by Mail: A
Guide to Houses from Sears, Roebuck and Company*. Washington,
D.C.: Preservation Press, 1986.
Synge, Jane. 'Self Help and Neighbourliness: Patterns of Life in
Hamilton.' In *The Canadian Worker in the Twentieth Century*, ed.
Irving Abella and David Millar, 97–104. Toronto: Oxford Uni-
versity Press, 1978.

Chapter 5 The Growing Influence of the State

Armstrong, Alan H. 'Thomas Adams and the Commission of
Conservation.' In *Planning the Canadian Environment*, ed. L.O.
Gertler, 17–35. Montreal: Harvest House, 1968.
Bacher, John. *Keeping to the Marketplace: The Evolution of Canadian
Housing Policy*. Montreal and Kingston: McGill-Queen's Univer-
sity Press, 1993.
Bauer, Catherine. *Modern Housing*. Boston: Houghton Mifflin, 1934.
Bauman, John F., Roger Biles, and Kristin Szylvain, eds. *From
Tenements to the Taylor Homes: In Search of an Urban Housing
Policy in Twentieth-Century America*. University Park, Penn.: Penn
State University Press, 2000.
Belec, John. 'The Dominion Housing Act.' *Urban History Review*
25, 2 (1997): 53–69.
Canada. Advisory Committee on Reconstruction. *Final Report of
the Subcommittee on Housing and Community Planning*. Ottawa:
King's Printer, 1944.
Carver, Humphrey. *Compassionate Landscape*. Toronto: University
of Toronto Press, 1975.

Collin, J.-P. 'A Housing Model for Lower and Middle-Class Wage
   Earners in a Montreal Suburb: Saint-Léonard, 1955–1967.'
   Journal of Urban History 24,4 (1998): 468–90.
Delaney, Jill. 'The Garden Suburb of Lindenlea, Ottawa: A
   Model Suburb for the First Federal Housing Policy, 1918–
   1924.' *Urban History Review* 19,3 (1991): 151–65.
Ferguson, R.S. 'The National Building Code of Canada and Its
   Fire Prevention Provisions.' In *Fire Research and Fire Prevention*,
   ed. National Research Council Division of Building Research,
   46–50. Ottawa: Division of Building Research, 1958.
Field, Alexander James. 'Uncontrolled Land Development and
   the Duration of the Depression in the United States.' *Journal of
   Economic History* 52,4 (1992): 785–805.
Harris, Richard. 'Slipping Through the Cracks: The Origins of
   Aided Self-Help Housing, 1918–1953.' *Housing Studies* 14,3
   (1999): 281–309.
– 'Flattered but Not Imitated: The Nova Scotia Housing Com-
   mission, 1936–1973.' *Acadiensis* 31,1 (2001): 103–28.
Harris, Richard, and Tricia Shulist. 'Canada's Reluctant Housing
   Program: The Veterans' Land Act, 1942–1975.' *Canadian His-
   torical Review* 82,2 (2001): 253–82.
Hulchanksi, J. David. 'The Origins of Urban Land Use Planning
   in Ontario, 1900–1946.' Unpublished PhD thesis, University of
   Toronto, 1981.
– 'The 1935 Dominion Housing Act: Setting the Stage for a Per-
   manent Federal Presence in Canada's Housing Sector.' *Urban
   History Review* 15,1 (1986): 19–40.
Moore, Peter. 'Zoning and Planning: The Toronto Experience,
   1904–1970.' In *The Usable Urban Past*, ed. Alan F.J. Artibise and
   Gilbert Stelter, 316–42. Toronto: Macmillan, 1979.
Radford, Gail. *Modern Housing for America: Policy Struggles in the
   New Deal Era.* Chicago: University of Chicago Press, 1997
Saywell, John. *Housing Canadians: Essays on the History of Residen-
   tial Construction in Canada.* Ottawa: Economic Council of
   Canada, 1975.
Sendbuehler, M, and Jason Gilliland. '"... to produce the highest

type of manhood and womanhood": The Ontario Housing Act, 1919, and a New Suburban Ideal.' *Urban History Review* 26,2 (1998): 42–55.

Shulist, Tricia, and Richard Harris. '"Build Your Own Home": State-Assisted Self-Help Housing in Canada, 1942–1975.' *Planning Perspectives* 17 (2002): 345–72.

Simpson, Michael. *Thomas Adams and the Modern Planning Movement: Britain, Canada and the United States, 1900–1940.* London: Mansell, 1985.

Smith, John C., and W. Bruce MacKinnon. 'Handcuffed Housing.' *Maclean's* (15 April 1947): 7–8.

Wade, Jill. 'Wartime Housing Limited, 1941–1947: Canadian Housing Policy at the Crossroads.' *Urban History Review* 15,1 (1986): 41–60.

– *Houses for All: The Struggle for Social Housing in Vancouver, 1919–1950.* Vancouver: UBC Press, 1994.

Weaver, John. 'The Property Industry and Land Use Controls: The Vancouver Experience, 1910–1945.' *Plan Canada* 19,3/4 (1979): 211–25.

Chapter 6 The Rise of the Corporate Suburb, 1945–1960

Bacher, John C. 'Canadian Housing "Policy" in Perspective.' *Urban History Review* 15,1 (1986): 3–18.

Buzzelli, Michael. 'Firm Size Structure in North American Housebuilding: Persistent Deconcentration, 1945–98.' *Environment and Planning, A* 33 (2001): 533–50.

Canada. Central Mortgage and Housing Corporation. *Housing and Urban Growth in Canada.* Ottawa: CMHC, 1956.

Carver, Humphrey. *Houses for Canadians: A Study of Housing Problems in the Toronto Area.* Toronto: University of Toronto Press, 1948.

– 'Building the Suburbs: A Planner's Reflections.' *City Magazine* 3,7 (1978): 40–5.

Choko, Marc. *Une Cité-Jardin à Montréal : La Cité-Jardin du Tricentenaire, 1940–1947.* Montreal: Méridien, 1989.

Choko, Marc, Jean-Pierre Collin, and Annick Germain. 'Le Loge-

ment et les Enjeux de la transformation de l'espace urbain :
Montréal, 1940–1960. Deuxième partie.' *Urban History Review,*
15,3 (1986): 243–53.

Clayton Research Associates. *The Housing Industry: Perspective and
Prospective.* Ottawa: CMHC, 1989. [Five Working Papers and
Final Report].

Colantonio, Frank. *From the Ground Up: An Italian Immigrant's
Story.* Toronto: Between the Lines, 1997.

Dugan, James. 'We Live in the World's Most Famous House.'
Maclean's 65 (1 May 1952): 10–11.

Filion, Pierre, and M. Alexander. 'Hidden Obstacles: Restrictive
Covenants as Impediments to Planning Objectives.' *Plan
Canada* 35,1 (1995): 33–7.

Garner, Hugh. 'You Take the Suburbs ... I Don't Want Them.'
Maclean's (10 Nov. 1954): 71–5.

Gray, John. 'Why Live in the Suburbs?' *Macleans* (1 Sept. 1954),
7–11.

Harris, Richard. 'From "Black-Balling" to "Marking": The Suburban Origins of Redlining in Canada, 1930s–1950s.' *Canadian
Geographer* 47,3 (2003): 338–50.

Holdsworth, Deryck. 'Metropolitan Toronto.' In *Historical Atlas of
Canada.* Vol. 3. *Addressing the Twentieth Century, 1891–1961,* ed.
Donald Kerr and Deryck Holdsworth, Plate 60. Toronto: University of Toronto Press, 1990.

Lorimer, Peter. *The Developers.* Toronto: Lorimer, 1976.

McKellar, James. 'Building Technology and the Production Process.' In *House, Home, and Community: Progress in Housing Canadians, 1945–1986,* ed. John Miron, 136–54. Montreal and
Kingston: McGill-Queen's University Press, 1993.

Pocius, Gerald. *A Place to Belong: Community Order and Everyday
Space in Calvert, Newfoundland.* Montreal and Kingston: McGill-
Queen's University Press, 1991.

Russell, Franklin. 'Let's Stop Building $15,000 Shacks.' *Maclean's*
36 (3 March 1956): 7.

Sileika, Antanas. *Buying on Time.* Erin, Ont.: Porcupine's Quill,
1997.

Walker, James W. St G. *'Race,' Rights and the Law in the Supreme Court of Canada.* Historical Case Studies. Toronto: Osgoode Society and Waterloo University Press, 1997.

Chapter 7 Creeping Conformity?

Cohen, Lizabeth. *Making a New Deal: Industrial Workers in Chicago, 1919–1939.* New York: Cambridge University Press.

Cowan, Ruth. *More Work for Mother: The Ironies of Household Technology from the Open Hearth to the Microwave.* New York: Basic Books, 1983.

Cromley, Elizabeth. 'Transforming the Food Axis: Houses, Tools, Modes of Analysis.' *Material History Review* 44 (1996): 8–19.

Davis, Donald. 'Competition's Moment: The Jitney-Bus and Corporate Capitalism in the Canadian City, 1914–1929.' *Urban History Review* 18,2 (1989): 103–22.

Edsall, Richard. 'This Changing Canada: Canadians Are on the Move.' *Canadian Business* 27 (Nov. 1954): 44–6.

Evenden, Leonard. 'Fleetwood in Surrey: The Making of a Place.' In *British Columbia: Geographical Essays Published in Honour of A. MacPherson,* ed. Paul M. Koroscil, 223–79. Burnaby, B.C.: Simon Fraser University Department of Geography.

Gendron, Y. 'Le destin parallèle de deux petites villes de Banlieue : Shawinigan-Sud et Trois Rivières-Ouest en Mauricie, 1945–1975.' *Revue d'histoire de l'Amérique Française* 52,4: 533–61.

Hobbs, Margaret, and Ruth Roach Pierson. '"A Kitchen that Wastes no Steps": Gender, Class and the Home Improvement Plan, 1936–1940.' *Histoire Sociale / Social History* 21 (1988): 9–37.

Ley, David F. 'Past Elites and Present Gentry: Neighbourhoods of Privilege in the Inner City.' In *The Changing Social Geography of Canadian Cities,* ed. Larry S. Bourne and David F. Ley, 214–33. Montreal and Kingston: McGill-Queen's University Press, 1993).

Marsh, Margaret. *Suburban Lives.* New Brunswick, N.J.: Rutgers University Press, 1990.

Miller, Roger. 'Household Activity Patterns in Nineteenth

Century Suburbs: A Time-Geographic Exploration.' *Annals of the Association of American Geographers* 72,3 (1982): 355–71.

Murdie, Robert A. 'Factorial Ecology of Metropolitan Toronto, 1951–1961.' University of Chicago, Department of Geography Research Paper No.116, 1969.

Ross, Mary. 'The Higher Conformity.' *Saturday Night* (18 July 1950): 31–2.

Index

Where suburbs are listed by name, the adjacent city is indicated in parentheses. Italics indicate a map or other illustration

Adams, Thomas, 76, 107–8
advertising: real estate, 52–3, *86*, 96, 142, 165
African-Americans, 42, 78, 88, 132
Africville (Halifax), 78, 100
Afro-Canadians, 78
Aladdin Company, 96
Ames, Herbert, 55, 82
Anderson, Kay, 87
anglophones: in Montreal, 29
Annex, The (Toronto), 8, *61*
annexation, *4*, 23, 66, 90; questioned, 72–3, 129, 153
anonymity of city life, 50–1
apartment buildings, 26, 52; concern about, 33–4, 36
architecture. *See* housing, styles of
Arnold, Mary, 114
assessment records, 78
Aurora (Toronto), 5

Australia, compared with Canada, 11, 40–1, 42, 148
automobiles, 7, 53, 159; effects on suburbs, 10, 18, 64, 68–9, 149, 168, 170–1; numbers of, 44, 63, 129–30, 162–3

Bacher, John, 143
Barton Township (Hamilton), 62, 72, 154
Baskerville, Peter, 52, 54
Bauer, Catherine, 112
B.C. Mills (company), 96
Beaver Lumber, 151
Belec, John, 120
Brantford, 151
British immigrants, 80, 87
British Properties, The (West Vancouver), 68
builders, 5, 11, 31, 93–9, 105, 117, 153; custom, 96–8, 100; speculative, 94–6, *97*, 100,

101, 123, 140–3. *See also*
owner-builders
building industry, 122; level of
activity, 112, 129, 162; organization of, 111, 113, 121,
123, 144–8
building materials, 152, 163;
innovations, 126, 141, 144–
5, 149
building permits, 158
building regulations: private,
85–7, 93, 99–100, 137–8;
municipal, 101, 109, 138,
149; – effects, 100, 144, 146,
153; national standards,
106, 126–7, 153, 169; – effects, 10, 106, 135
Burgess, E.W., 61
Burnaby (Vancouver), 42,
136
Buzzelli, Michael, 145

Calgary, 70–1, 111, 144; land
speculation, 91; suburbs, 48,
71, 73, 87, 140, 149; transit, 9
Canada Mortgage and Hous-
ing Corporation. *See* Central Mortgage and Housing
Corporation
Canadian Pacific Railway
(CPR), 71, 75; as land
owner, 48, 71
Carver, Humphrey, 15, 121,
131, 143
Casa Loma, 99
Catholic Church: in Quebec,
32, 115

census tracts, 77
Central Business District
(CBD), 61
Central (now Canada) Mort-
gage and Housing Corpora-
tion (CMHC), 120–1, 123,
134–6; development stand-
ards, 135–7, 143, 153
children, 27, 35; importance
of suburbs for, 14, 30–1, 33,
76, 125, 165–6; in suburbs,
3, 40, 44, 45, 51, 160, 172
Chinese immigrants, 87
Choko, Marc, 29
churches: in suburbs, 40, 80,
125, 165
Cité-Jardin de Tricentenaire
(Montreal), 32, 37, 115
Clark, S.D., 7, 23, 39–41
Clark, W.C., 113
Cobalt, Ont., 100
Cohen, Lizabeth, 161
Colantonio, Frank, 140, 145
Coldbrook Garden City (Saint
John), 47
Commission of Conservation,
107, 108
community organizations, 37–
42, 51–2, 163
commuting. *See* journey to
work
conformity. *See* suburbs, conformity in
consumerism, 32; class convergence, 161–5; in corporate
suburbs, 5, 7, 17, 132, 164–5,
172–4

Cooperative Commonwealth
  Federation (CCF), 5, 42, 51,
  118
Copp, Terry, 31, 53
corporate suburbs: character
  of, 5, 152, 159, 164–6, 172–4;
  examples, 138, 140; making
  of, 123, 128, 129–33, 135,
  136–48, 153–4, 168
country, the, 20, 40, 43, 46, 48
covenants. See land, private
  regulation of
credit. See debt; mortgages
Curtis, C.A., 115
Curtis Report, 115, 116, 123

Dalzell, A.G., 90, 91
Davis, Donald, 12, 67, 70, 171
debt, 32, 43, 104, 132
deed restrictions. See land, private regulation of
Dennis, Richard, 34
department stores, 122, 131
Diamond, Etan, 39
do-it-yourself, 35, 152, 164
domestic appliances, 158–9,
  160, 161, 163
domesticity: in suburbs, 14, 30,
  33; valuation of, 7, 34
Dominion Housing Act. See
  housing policy
Don Mills (Toronto), 24, 38;
  developed as corporate suburb, 137–8, 148
Doucet, Michael, 28, 74, 79,
  84, 138
Douglass, Harlan, 49

Dovercourt Land, Building
  and Savings Company, 89

East Calgary, 71
East End (Montreal), 58, 75,
  135, 136
East Kildonan (Winnipeg), 62,
  68
East York (Toronto), 61, 136;
  annexation rebuffed, 72,
  110; politics in, 42; tax
  arrears, 93
Eaton Company, T., 96, 122
Eburne (Vancouver), 38
Edel, Matthew, 27, 31–2
Edmonton: land speculation,
  91, 92–3; suburbs, 48, 64,
  65, 73, 87, 136, 140; transit
  in, 9
elite suburbs, 65, 153; character, 20–1, 71–2; examples,
  20; making of, 68, 71, 99–
  100, 109; as suburbs, 19, 24,
  102–3, 130
Elliott, Bruce, 63, 127
Elmwood (Winnipeg), 59, 62;
  British immigrants in, 80;
  development, 100; transit,
  64
environmental movement, 37
ethnic identity, 38–9. See also
  immigrants
Etobicoke (Toronto), 38
Evans, Arthur (owner-
  builder), 3, 4, 10, 23, 42,
  104, 111
Evenden, Leonard, 163

families: extended, 54; importance of suburbs for, 25–6,
36, 51–2, 125, 166; nuclear,
14, 17; in suburbs, 12, 40,
43, 149–50
Federal Housing Administration (FHA) (U.S.), 119–21,
123, 132
feminists, 167, 168; on suburbs, 14, 44
Fishman, Robert, 20, 21
Fleetwood (Vancouver), 163
Foran, Max, 70
Forest Hill (Toronto), 12, *61*;
as elite suburb, 20, 72, 157;
housing, 120, 142; incorpo-
ration, 72; Jewish settlement, 80, 89
Fort William (now Thunder
Bay), 90
francophones: in Montreal,
29, 52

Galt, Ont., 20
Garden City: idea of, 46, 107;
in Canada, *47*, 60, 93, 99,
108, 115
Garner, Hugh, 15
ghettoes, 87, 131
Glenora (Edmonton), *65*
Goad insurance atlases, 97
Gray, John, 12, 24, 25
Great Britain, 62, 81; housing
policy, 112; planning legisla-
tion, 106–7; suburbs in, 20,
22, 25, 48, 76, 172
Great Depression, effects on:

attitude to debt, 165; building, 112; evolution of corporate suburb, 128; foreclosures, 3, 111; housing finance, 10–11, 105, 111, 128;
politics, 42; post-war demand, 129, 149, 162

Halifax, N.S., 49, 57, 101, 146
Hall, Peter, 46
Hamilton: annexations by, 72,
153–4; builders in, 141, 142–
3; housing, 26, 28, 54, 108,
118, 120; mortgages, 133–4,
135; segregation in, 74, 79,
82; suburbs, 62, 101, *135*,
136; transit, 65, 70
Hampstead Garden Suburb
(London, England), 90
Hastings, Charles, 53
health: in cities, 30–1, 52–6,
57; in suburbs, 92, 155,
169
Henderson, Harry, 38, 39, 43–
4
Hiebert, Dan, 78, 79
Hintonburg (Ottawa), 63, 92,
100
Hodgetts, Charles, 107
Holdsworth, Deryck, 102
Home and School associa-
tions, 37
Home Owners' Loan Corpo-
ration (HOLC) (U.S.),
127–8
home ownership, 19; aspirations for, 26–9, 170; levels

of, 26, 28–9; political effects, 5, 36, 41–3
housework, 28, 34, 158–60,
housing: conditions, 35, 55, 56–7, 81; crowding, 52, 54–5, 56; financing, 7, 10, 16, 104–5, 119–23, 133–6, 153; as investment, 27, 28, 33, 36; plexes, 34; shortages, 129–48; single family, 18, 25–6, 29, 34–6; styles of, before 1939, 94, 95, 102, 108, 156–7, 160; – after 1939, 122, 130, 144, 163–4, 173. See also apartment buildings; builders; building industry; home ownership; lodging; mortgages
housing policy: after 1918, 41, 107–8; aided self-help, 107, 116–19, 171; and suburbs, 32, 132–3; cooperatives, 113–16; Dominion Housing Act (DHA), 11, 119–20, 127, 128, 132–3, 134; Home Improvement Plan, 162; National Housing Act (NHA), 11, 120–1, 123, 126, 143, 153; public housing, 112–13, 115, 119, 171. See also CMHC; Veterans Land Act
Howard, Ebenezer, 46
Hudson's Bay Company: as land owner, 48, 65, 87
Hulchanski, David, 108
Hydrostone district (Halifax), 101, 161

Iacovetta, Franca, 13
immigrants, 78, 80; prejudice against, 87; in suburbs, 14, 27–8; – before 1939, 5, 23, 40, 42, 62, 66, 159–60, 165; – after 1945, 131, 149–50
immigration: and population growth, 9, 50, 54; and building industry, 146–7, 149–50
individualism, 23, 52, 74
industrial growth, 23, 52, 74; decentralization, 56–62, 70–1
industrial suburbs, 153; character of, 60, 101, 109; examples, 23; making of, 58–62, 101; prevalence of, 103; as suburbs, 23, 49
Irish immigrants, 28
Italian immigrants, 28, 87, 131, 146–7

Jackson, Kenneth T., 20–1, 22, 132
Jacques Cartier, Ville (Montreal), 24
Jewish immigrants, 28, 55, 78, 80, 87, 88, 131; in suburbs, 39, 89
jitneys, 67, 69–70, 171
journey to work, 19, 30, 171; before 1939, 9, 60, 63, 68–9, 102, 159–60; after 1945, 69

Kerrisdale (Vancouver), 102
Kingsway Park (Toronto): development of, 68, 88–9,

96, 120, 142, 147; as elite
suburb, 68
Kitchener, 69, 127
kitchens, 158–9, 162
kit houses, 95–6, 151
Korinek, Valerie, 13

Lachine (Montreal), 29, *61*,
62
land developers, 5, 17, 31, 58,
64; of corporate suburbs,
10; install services, 137–9;
use of restrictions, 36, 93;
vertical integration, 75, 137,
140–3, 145
land development, 17, 75, 112;
before 1939, 62, 63–4, 70–1,
83–93; after 1945, 137–41,
148, 153. *See also* land subdivision
land, private regulation of:
architectural controls, 100,
137–8; building regula-
tions, 85–7, 93, 137–8; ethnic covenants, 87–9, 93, 100;
zoning, 138
land, public regulation of:
subdivision controls, 10,
106, 108, 110, 123–4, 135,
137, 169; zoning, 10, 36, 50,
86, 108, 124–5, 137–8, 153
land registry, 133
land speculation, 10, 84, 90–3,
139
land subdivision, 8, 16, 83–
103, 105, 111, 121, 138. *See
also* subdivision design

Lawrence Park (Toronto), 20,
64, 85, 89
League of Catholic Workers,
32–3, 115
Leaside (Toronto), 23, *61*, 69;
annexation rebuffed, 72;
industry, 23, 60; subdivision
design, 60
leisure, 35, 39, 157
Lethbridge, Alta., *139*
Levitt, William, 12, 141–2
Lewis, Robert, 12, 57, 79
Ley, David, 156
Lindenlea (Ottawa), 108
Linteau, Paul-André, 58
London, England, 35, 62, 172
Longeuil (Montreal), 43, *44*,
146
Lorimer, James, 15, 17
lumber dealers, 122, 141, 153;
response to owner builders,
150–2, 164

Macphail, Agnes, 42
Maisonneuve (Montreal), 58,
59, 62, 65, 101
malls, 130, *131*, 138
Mansur, David, 121, 135
Marsh, Margaret, 28, 159
mass suburbs. *See* corporate
suburbs
Massey-Harris (company), 57
McCall, Edith, 26–7, 28–9, 103
McCann, L.D., 12
Melbourne, Australia, 41
men: as builders, 93, 147–8,
149–50, 159; as commuters,

30, 44, 130, 166; in homes,
157, 159, 167; in suburbs,
14, 30
metropolitan government, 22,
126
Michelson, William, 35–6
middle-class suburbs: character of, 102, 109, 158–9, 161–
2; examples, 89, 102; making of, 87–8, 102; as suburbs, 5, 9
middle class, 6; housing of,
27–9
Mississauga (Toronto), 142
Montreal, 9, 49, 57, *59*; developers, 140, 146; govern-
ment, 22; health, 53–4;
housing, 26, 27, 29, 34, 52,
82, 126; housing finance,
135; immigrants, 88; labour
force participation of wom-
en, 30, 167–8; segregation
in, 78–9; suburbs, 6, 8, 24,
30, *59*, 61, 62, 149
Moore, Peter, 36, 84, 124
mortality, 30–1, 53–4, 55, 81
mortgages, 103–4, 119–21,
133–6, 154; amortization,
11, 19, 164; balloon, 11,
103–4; dependence on, 10,
98, 103; foreclosures, 3, 111;
individual, 3, 10, 104–5, 136;
institutional, 32, 104–5,
119–21, 128, 133–6, 143, 171;
redlining, 133–136, 148
Morton, Suzanne, 14, 161
Mount Dennis (Toronto), 69

Mount Royal (Calgary), 71, 99
Mount Royal (Montreal): as
elite suburb, 20, 62–3, 99,
135
municipal finances, 92–3,
110–11
municipal franchise, 37, 124
municipal government: in cities, 109; and suburban identity, 19, 22, 24, 71–3; in suburbs, 22, 58, 126
municipal services, 52; in cities, 109; in suburbs, 81, 84,
99–100, 156, 163; – cost
of, 91–2, 109–10, 169; – installed by developers, 137–9,
140, 141, 154; – lack of, 38,
68

National Housing Act (NHA).
See housing policy
National Policy, 49
National Research Council,
127
Neighbourhood Unit, 125,
139, 165
neighbours, 56, 81; in sub-
urbs, 40–1, 44
Nepean (Ottawa), 63, 91, 127
Newfoundland, 151
New Toronto (Toronto): as
industrial suburb, 23, 59, 60,
61, 69, 75
New Urbanism, 170
NIMBY (not-in-my-backyard)
syndrome, 37
North End (Winnipeg), as

industrial suburb, 23, 62;
immigrants, 80, 82; politics,
42, 82
North York (Toronto), 38,
127, 137
Noseworthy, Joseph, 5, 42
Nova Scotia Housing Commission, 114–15, 119

Olmsted, John, 46–8, 64, 86,
87, 99
Olson, Sherry, 52, 81
Ottawa, 136, 140
Outremont (Montreal). 20,
29, 31, 72
owner-builders: before 1929,
3, 5, 23, 42, 61; – building
methods, 98–9; after 1945,
44, 117, 160–1, 163; – building methods, 148–53, 163–4;
Canada and U.S. compared,
103, 105

Parkdale (Toronto), 69
Park Royal (North Vancou-
ver), 131
Parsons Estate (Toronto), 87,
89, 165
Paterson, Ross, 85, 96
Pearson, Norman, 18, 48,
167
philanthropic housing, 55–6
Pigott, Joseph, 121–2
Piva, Michael, 53
planning: provincial legislation, 106, 108, 123–6;
municipal, 124–6

Point Douglas (Winnipeg),
23, 62, 64
Point Grey (Vancouver), 20,
72, 90, 102
pollution, 30–1, 52–3, 125
porches, 162, 163
Port Arthur (now Thunder
Bay), 151
prefabrication, 146
Prince Albert, 87
Prince George, 87
Prince Rupert, 87
privacy: in suburbs, 35, 172; on
public transit, 67; valuation
of, 7, 25–6, 34–5, 55, 67
Progressive Conservative
Party, 5
provincial governments: subdivision controls, 106, 108;
suburban government, 22,
126; suburban planning,
106, 123–6, 128
public health initiatives, 53,
55, 109
public transit, 56, 62–7; buses,
67, 68; horsecars, 9, 53, 62;
jitneys, 67, 69–70, 171; railways, 57, 58, 59, 62–3; streetcars, 4, 30, 53, 159, 161, 170;
– effects on suburbs, 8–9,
63–71, 167

Quebec, 5–6, 32–3
Quebec City, 22, 74

Randle, Alice, 24, 100–1, 160,
166

real estate agents, 36
Relph, Edward, 125
retailing, 37, 39, 80, 81, 167,
    173; home delivery, 159–60;
    malls, 130, *131*, 138
Rideau Heights (Kingston),
    103
Riis, Jacob, 82
River Heights (Winnipeg), 80
roads, 68–9, 130
Rosedale (Toronto), 20, *61*
Rowell, Thomas, 41
Rutherford, Paul, 55

Sackville, N.B., 115
Saywell, John, 91
schools: in suburbs, 37, 40,
    139, 157, 165–6
Sears, Roebuck and Company,
    96
Seeley, John, 12, 164
segregation, 36, 87; of classes,
    77–80, 81–3; defined, 76–7;
    of ethnic groups, 80–1; of
    land uses, 74–5, 125
servants, 28, 30, 157, 158, 167
Sewell, John, 125
shacks, 98–9, 100, 110–11,
    149
shacktowns, 23, 24, 149, 159,
    165. *See also* unplanned sub-
    urbs
Shaughnessy Heights (Van-
    couver), *21*; architectural
    controls, 100; as elite sub-
    urb, 20, 64, 92
Sifton, Clifford, 107

Silverthorn Park (Vancouver),
    85–6, 101
slums, 31, 35, 44, 46, 67, 76;
    discourse of, 56, 155
Smith, Peter, 64
social class, 67, 77, 159; defini-
    tion of, 21; and suburbs, 24,
    27. *See also* middle class;
    workers
South Vancouver, 3, 80;
    annexation of, 72; develop-
    ment, 100; land speculation,
    90–1; politics, 42
St-Boniface (Winnipeg), 60
St-Léonard (Montreal), 32–3,
    37, 40, 115
Stockholm: housing, 116,
    171
Strathcona (Edmonton),
    92–3
St Urbain (Montreal), 80
streetcars. *See* public transit
Strong-Boag, Veronica, 44–5,
    150, 167
subdivision design, 84, *86*, 102,
    117, 139, 165
suburbanites, 7
suburbanization, 6, 8–12;
    causes, 56–71; conse-
    quences, political, 41–3;
    – social 7–8, 14, 33–45;
    – unintended, 33–45;
    early history, 48–9; timing,
    6, 8–12, 129
suburban way of life, 12–3, 18,
    24–45, 155–73
suburbia, 130–1

suburbs: Canadian distinctive,
19, 21–2; conformity in 7,
39; density, 18, 24, 31, 71,
130, 170; diversity among,
7–8, 14, 16–17, 74, 106, 131–
2, 160–1; – within, 100; government of, 22, 58, 106, 126;
historiography, 12–17, 22;
homogeneity among, 16,
24–5, 130–2, 143–4, 155,
173–4; – within, 74, 95, 102;
physical aspects, 18–24, 40–
1, 99; redlining, 133–6; residential character, 19, 22, 30,
49; types, 22–3, 99–105. See
also corporate –; elite –;
industrial –; middle-class –;
unplanned
Supreme Court of Canada,
89
Swansea (Toronto), 72
synagogues, 39

tax arrears, 93, 110–11, 169
Taylor, E.P., 137
tenants, 26, 37, 110, 123, 124
Thompson, F.M.L., 15, 48
Thorncrest Village (Toronto),
37–8, 39, 172
Thornhill (Toronto), 38
Thornton, Patricia, 81
thrift, 164–5
Tomkinsville, N.S., 114
tools: for building, 145, 147,
149, 152
Toronto, 9, 61; annexation by,
66, 72; building in, 97, 126;

government of, 22, 61, 126;
housing, 26, 34, 35, 54, 55–
6, 108, 158; immigrants, 55,
80, industry, 57–8, 60, 61,
74; segregation in, 78; suburbs, 8, 24, 40, 60, 61, 100;
transit, 69, 70, 170; zoning,
36
Toronto Housing Company,
55–6
Toronto Railway Company,
10, 65–6
Transcona (Winnipeg), 59,
62, 64, 90
Tuxedo (Winnipeg), 20, 64

L'Union économique d'habitations (UED), 32
Union Park (Hamilton), 89
United States compared with
Canada: automobiles, 68;
building industry, 145; city-
suburban contrasts, 75–6;
housing finance, 104–5,
111–12, 119–21, 123; housing policy, 112–15, 119; land
development, 141–2; lodg-
ing, 54; municipal government, 22, 72; owner-
building, 148; politics, 41,
42; segregation, 77–8, 88,
124, 170; slums, 56, 76;
streetcars, 63, 66; suburbanization, 11, 16; types of suburbs, 16, 103, 132
unplanned suburbs, 130, 153;
as suburbs, 23–4; character,

76, 100–1, 159, 168–9; examples, 100; making of, 100–1, 105, 152, 159; prevalence of, 23, 103, 148
Uplands, The (Victoria), 20, *86*; subdivision design, 48, 64, *86*, 87; transit, 64
urbanity, 29, 50
urbanization: consequences, 50–6; of Canada, 5, 9, 49–56
urban reformers, 52, 55, 56

Vallières, Pierre, 5–6, 43, *44*, 166
Vancouver, *4*, 57; annexations by, 3, *4*, 72, 90; housing, 120; land, 87; suburbs, 3, 48; transit, 9; zoning, 124
van Nus, Walter, 88
veterans, housing for: after 1918, 41, 107–8; after 1945, 116–19, 123
Veterans Land Act, 120; as housing program, 116–19, 149, 150, 171

walking, 9
Ward, The (Toronto), 55, *61*, 80
Warner, Sam Bass, 63
Wartime Housing, 121–3
Waterloo Township, 69
Weaver, John, 12, 28, 38, 55, 79, 86, 88, 94, 124, 138
Weiss, Marc, 17
Westdale (Hamilton), 20; building, 94, *95*, 147; character, 89, 102; planning, 93, 138; subdivision, 83–4, 88
West End (Vancouver), 157
West Kildonan (Winnipeg), 80
Westmount (Montreal), 20, 157; annexation resisted, 72; health, 31; housing, 29, 135; land regulation, 100
West Toronto Junction (Toronto), 23, 59, *61*, 74, 101
West Vancouver, 68, 131, 140
Wetherell, Donald, 149
Wilmington, Dela, 89
Winch, Ernest, 42
Windsor, 143
Winnipeg: General Strike, 82; housing, 26–7; land, 87; segregation in, 78–9, 80; suburbs, 48, 80; transit, 9, 70
Wirth, Louis, 50
women: as builders, 150–1; as investors, 84, 104; in homes, 28, 34, 157–60; in labour force, 30, 148, 167; single, 30, 34; on streetcars, 67; in suburbs, 30, 43–4, 156–7, 159–60, 166–8, 170
Woodsworth, J.S., 51, 55, 67, 83
workers, 6; in suburbs, before 1939, 5, 23, 27–8, 41–3, 62, 66, 159–61; – after 1945, 131, 162–4; politics of, 14, 41–2, 57, 82
York Township (Toronto), *61*;

annexation rebuffed, 72, 110; development of, 87, 100, 107, 127, 136; industry, 23, 60, *61*, 153; politics, 42; services, 92, 100; tax arrears, 93; transit, 66; as unplanned suburb, 80, 87, 100

zoning. *See* land, public regulation of

THEMES IN CANADIAN HISTORY

Editors:
Craig Heron 1997–
Franca Iacovetta 1997–1999

1 Paul Axelrod, *The Promise of Schooling: Education in Canada,
1800–1914*
2 Carolyn Strange and Tina Loo, *Making Good: Law and Moral
Regulation in Canada, 1867–1939*
3 Allan Greer, *The People of New France*
4 Cynthia R. Comacchio, *The Infinite Bonds of Family: Domesticity in
Canada, 1850–1940*
5 Sarah Carter, *Aboriginal People and Colonizers of Western Canada
to 1900*
6 Colin D. Howell, *Blood, Sweat, and Cheers: Sport and the Making of
Modern Canada*
7 Richard Harris, *Creeping Conformity: How Canada Became Suburban, 1900–1960*